Coping with

AN ABUSIVE RELATIONSHIP

Carlene Cobb

The Rosen Publishing Group, Inc.
New York

With special thanks to my son, Michael Tozian, for his courageous independence; I dedicate this book to the memory of victims who did not survive violence, to the survivors who walk away from abuse, and to all those who help others.

Published in 2001 by The Rosen Publishing Group, Inc.
29 East 21st Street, New York, NY 10010

First Edition

Cover photo © Dave Ryan/IndexStock

Library of Congress Cataloging-in-Publication Data

Cobb, Carlene.
Coping with an abusive relationship / by Carlene Cobb.
p. cm. — (Coping)
Includes bibliographical references and index.
ISBN 0-8239-2822-5 (library binding)
1. Abused teenagers—Juvenile literature. [1. Family violence. 2. Dating violence. 3. Violence.] I. Title. II. Series.
RJ507.A29 C63 2001
616.85'82'00835—dc21

2001001728

Manufactured in the United States of America

Contents

Introduction

Adolescence, at times, can feel like a roller coaster ride. You have to deal with unexpected ups and downs and twists and turns. For teens trying to cope with an abusive relationship, the roller coaster ride is even more traumatic. A relationship that starts out exhilarating and exciting can become exhausting, frightening, shaming, and dangerous. A sunlit stroll in the park can, without warning, turn into a thundering storm of criticism, accusations, threats, bruising blows, or forced sex.

Abusive relationships are the leading cause of injury to women between the ages of fifteen and forty-four. They occur at all income levels, and among all ethnic groups, and in both straight and gay relationships. Abusers can be parents, stepparents, other caregivers or family members, bullies, and dating partners. It is important to remember that nobody deserves abuse. Abuse of any kind must be taken seriously, not denied, minimized, or excused. This is true whether the weapons used are words or fists. Anyone can be a victim, though certain circumstances increase an individual's likelihood of abusing others and/or being abused. Those risk factors are discussed in this book.

1

A teen living at home with an abusive parent may need to devise a safety plan focused on retreating to another part of the house, escaping to a friend's home, not reacting, even dropping to the floor and curling up in a ball to deflect physical injury. Because the teen is legally dependent upon the parent, trying every method to work out the problem through family counseling and other supportive social services is desirable. If the situation is unsafe, Child Protection Services (CPS) may intervene and remove the teen from the home, but every effort is made to improve the situation and keep the family intact. The steps in the processes for both options are discussed in this book.

Conversely, a teen facing abusive peer groups and dating partners more often needs to gain self-respect, speak up, take a stand, set boundaries, and end the relationship(s). In either case, teens face tough choices. This book discusses how teens can find help in processing these difficult decisions and safely take action.

Counselors who work with abused and abusive teens emphasize the importance of the following actions:

- Break the silence by telling a trusted adult or friend about the abuse.

- Create a safety plan whether you decide you need to stay or leave the relationship.

- Learn to eliminate self-blame and nurture self-esteem.

The first step is to recognize abusive situations. Some victims of abuse have lived with maltreatment all their lives and regard it as normal. To help distinguish between healthy and abusive behaviors, abuse is defined and symptoms indicating potentially abusive personalities are identified in this book.

More Common Than You May Think

Research shows that adolescents experience maltreatment at rates equal to or exceeding those of younger children, with an overall rate of 25.7 cases per 1,000 persons age twelve to seventeen. The most recent large-scale study of adolescent health and well-being in the United States, the 1997 Commonwealth Fund survey on the Health of Adolescent Girls, revealed that one in five high school girls (20 percent) and one in eight boys (13 percent) surveyed reported physical or sexual abuse by the age of eighteen. Physical and sexual abuse of girls was most likely to happen in the home (53 percent), occur more than once (65 percent), and be perpetrated by family members (57 percent) or family friends (13 percent). Physical abuse of boys also was most likely to occur in the home (66 percent) and be perpetrated by a family member (68 percent). Only 35 percent of sexual abuse of boys occurred at home, and 45 percent was perpetrated by a family member.

In a self-reported, anonymous survey at a co-ed high school in California, abused and nonabused girls indicated concerns about violence at home: One in four said she wanted to leave home at some time because of the violence. Of the girls who reported experiencing domestic violence, 58 percent said they wanted to leave home at some point because of violence and not feeling safe there.

Different Types of Abuse

Emotional abuse is defined as any behavior, language, or attitude that interferes with a person's self-esteem, mental health, or social development. It is as devastating as physical abuse, even though the injury is invisible. Examples of emotional abuse include raging, yelling, belittling, criticizing, intimidating with verbal threats, and name-calling. Unless some type of intervention stops these behaviors, emotional and verbal abuse often escalate to physical abuse.

Physical abuse is any injury or series of injuries appearing to be nonaccidental in nature. Parents who choose physical punishment as a disciplinary action risk crossing the line between discipline and abuse, particularly during times of high stress. Examples of physical abuse include slapping, shoving, punching, and beating with an object. Even tickling a person relentlessly and beyond requests to stop can be physically abusive. If the teen strikes back when attacked by the abuser, the fact that the physical abuse has become mutual does not make it acceptable behavior.

Sexual abuse is defined legally as any sexual act between an adult and a minor (a person under eighteen years of age). However, it can also occur between teens who are both minors. The perpetrator of sexual abuse may be a stranger but is more often a parent, stepparent, sibling, or other family member, caregiver, or close family friend. Sexual abuse of teenage girls typically occurs at home and is not an isolated incident. Sexual abuse of boys more often occurs away from home. Dating violence (or date rape) and sexual coercion are other forms of sexual abuse among teens.

If the abuser is a family member, the teen may be afraid that exposing the abuse will destroy the family, and it does seriously impact the family. But keeping the secret can ultimately destroy the teen. Telling a friend about an abusive dating relationship can be embarrassing, but the teen must choose self-preservation over staying with a boyfriend or girlfriend who is abusive.

Healthy relationships are based on love, mutual respect, and encouraging each other's interests and goals. This is true of healthy relationships between teens and parents, friends, and dating partners.

Symptoms of Emotional, Physical, and Sexual Abuse

Symptoms of emotional, physical, or sexual abuse you may notice in yourself or a friend include:

- ❧ Bruises, cuts, abrasions, broken bones, limping

- ❧ Signs of depression, including altered sleep patterns and weight gain or loss

- ❧ Mention of suicide or self-harm (self-inflicted cuts, burns, food deprivation)

- ❧ Eating disorders, such as anorexia, bulimia, and compulsive eating

- ❧ Difficulty getting along with one's peers and/or authority figures

⮞ Problems with handling anger

⮞ Sudden drop in grades at school

⮞ Withdrawal from friends or hanging with a different crowd

⮞ Dropping out of activities once enjoyed

⮞ School truancy

⮞ Promiscuity

⮞ Brushes with the law, including stealing, vandalism, and underage drinking

⮞ Experimentation with drugs or alcohol

⮞ Runaway behavior

Not all teens who exhibit one or more of these symptoms are victims of abuse, but the first three especially need to be taken seriously and responded to appropriately. Any time a teen mentions suicide, the situation needs to be reported to a trusted adult. You can also call a teen hotline or crisis hotline. It is too risky to try to handle that situation without help.

Stop the Abuse

This book endeavors to assist teens in recognizing the differences between healthy and abusive relationships among family members, peer groups, and dating partners. If you are in an abusive relationship, reading this book will help you understand why it happens, what you can do to feel better, and how you can safely end the relationship when appropriate. If you think a friend is being abused, reading this book can help both of you support each other during this fragile process of growth and change. It is important to stay safe by taking any abuse seriously, and telling a trusted friend or adult what is happening. If you need immediate help, call the National Domestic Violence Hotline, (800) 799-SAFE (7233), (800) 787-3224 (TTY). This crisis line provides professional staff twenty-four hours a day to talk with you and make local referrals.

This book addresses abuse that happens to teens at home, among peers, in dating relationships, and with their intimate partners. Although teens experience diminished self-esteem and other similar adverse effects in all three types of abusive relationships, the coping skills needed for each situation differ.

Understanding Abusive Relationships

Life provides many learning and growth opportunities, and some lessons are painful. However, a "lesson" should never threaten your physical safety or mental and emotional well-being. Undergoing painful situations may hold some value—but only by demonstrating to you what you do not want in your life. Recognizing that you are being abused in your home is a big step. Awareness is the beginning of taking appropriate action.

The major points to remember are these:

➣ If you have been emotionally, physically, or sexually abused, you are not alone.

➣ What happened to you is not your fault. Do not blame yourself.

➣ There is more awareness and understanding of abusive behaviors today than ever before, and more programs are available to help you cope and stay safe.

Emotional Abuse

Abuse does not have to be physical to do harm. Emotional abuse is defined as any attitude or behavior that interferes with an individual's mental health or social development and could cause serious behavioral, cognitive, emotional, or mental problems. It is as damaging as physical abuse and often more difficult to identify. Thus, it can be a greater challenge to heal. The wounds inflicted by emotional abuse may be invisible, but they hurt for a long time. Emotional abuse attacks the person's character, not the deed allegedly committed.

Emotional abuse of teens occurs when parents rage, yell, intimidate with verbal threats, practice habitual scapegoating ("It's your fault I'm so upset . . . "), belittle, shame, make negative comparisons to others, and call the teen names. It also includes extreme forms of punishment, such as confining an individual and enforcing unreasonably prolonged periods of isolation and loss of freedom. In some cases of reported emotional abuse, the abuser's actions alone, whether or not harm is evident in the teen's behavior or condition, warrants the intervention of Child Protection Services. CPS and the Department of Children and Families are responsible for deciding if the child or teen needs to be removed from the home and placed in foster care until the home environment is deemed safe again.

Witnessing extreme anger, rage, and temper tantrums in the home upsets and injures everyone, whether or not they are directly involved. Even a baby in a high chair senses tension between people seated around the dinner table. Parents who think they are keeping their rage a secret from children of any age are deluding themselves.

9

Anger or Rage?

Rage is a shame-based, unhealthy expression of anger. It is characterized by screaming, throwing and breaking things, threatening violence, sulking, psychological manipulation, emotional blackmail, and trying to use anger to punish. It is one form of emotional abuse. Young children are terrified of raging parents, and teens, too, can be confused by rage and afraid of the rager. Victims tend to blame themselves when a loved one's storm of anger engulfs them. They feel helpless and desperate to fix the problem, though they have no idea how to do that.

Teens who are harshly criticized and berated may lack confidence and feel bad about themselves. They are less likely to try new things for fear of disapproval. They may find it hard to develop close relationships, feel discouraged in a variety of settings, and underachieve at school. No matter which family member is the target of the scolding, children and teens watch, experience, and learn how to rage. They associate their own shame with shaming others.

Why does rage happen and why does it recur? Rage sets up a neurochemical reaction in the brain of the abuser. This internal response can be addictive, producing what is known as rage-aholism. Raging gives the rager a feeling of power, finally being able to release feelings that were repressed for years. Because the rager may not have been allowed to communicate feelings as a child, he or she may have never learned a healthy means of expressing anger.

Anger is a natural emotion. Learning to manage your anger is a valid goal and one that promises great gifts: peace of mind and happier relationships.

Effects of Emotional Abuse

If you are a teen who has grown up in a volatile home environment, you are at increased risk of developing conflict resolution problems and perceiving your own inappropriate behaviors as normal. You may shout, sulk in silence, or develop a critical attitude. Judging yourself and others harshly leads to thinking negatively, isolating yourself, and alienating your peers—the very people whose acceptance you most wish to win.

Motivation and confidence problems associated with raging family members and other emotional abuse may surface at this time, impacting academic performance beyond the "middle school malaise" that often typifies the sixth- and seventh-grade experience. When grades drop and consequences are levied, you may lose privileges at school and home and feel the slipping of your popularity among classmates. This can further discourage you into a downward spiral.

Any form of emotional abuse can lead to long-term issues of self-esteem and profound emotional repercussions that may ruin present and future relationships of all types. And verbal abuse typically progresses into other forms. Wounding words may lead to more overt threats and physical abuse, particularly in stressful times. Partners and children of abusers, whether adults, teens, or young children, often think they somehow provoked the abuse, that they could have prevented it by saying or doing the right thing, that it is their fault. None of that is true.

Physical Abuse

Defined as any nonaccidental injury to a child or teen, physical abuse includes slapping, hitting, kicking, shaking, burning, pinching, hair-pulling, biting, choking, shoving, and striking with an object. Although parents are free to decide whether or not physical punishment is an appropriate option for disciplining their children, when the physical punishment is too harsh, the discipline crosses the line and becomes abuse. A parent who crosses that line may be reacting to his or her own stress level, justifying the action as a means to teach a lesson. Unfortunately, the only lesson demonstrated is the parent's loss of control.

A common contributing factor in physical abuse cases is a caretaker who is affected by drinking and drug abuse. Records suggest a link with alcohol or drug abuse in about 50 percent of violent attacks in the home, according to the Family Violence Prevention Fund. Teens who live with alcoholism and child abuse need to seek help for both problems. If alcohol or drug use complicates the abusive situation at home, both the addiction(s) and the abusive behaviors need to be addressed and treated.

Not all children who experience abusive behaviors at home become abusers or victims of violence. Many can be helped through family counseling, psychotherapy, support groups, and community organizations developed to address the specific needs of child abuse victims and their families. Children of violence are more likely to become involved in abusive relationships as teens and adults unless they learn how to break the cycle of abuse. The saying, "If you do not recover, you will repeat" is a good incentive to ask for help.

The Effects of Physical Abuse

Children who grow up witnessing or experiencing physical violence at home are at greater risk for becoming perpetrators of physical violence in their own relationships. Studies show that many children first fear violence, then they copy it. Children who are witnesses or victims of domestic violence may later exhibit hostility, aggression, and antisocial behavior, called "externalized" behaviors.

Other abuse victims are affected differently, exhibiting "internalized" behaviors. These internalized behaviors are exhibited by an individual who appears fearful, inhibited, depressed, hopeless, or unmotivated. Symptoms of physical abuse are bruises, abrasions, burns, cuts, or broken bones. Abusers may target body areas where bruises will not show unless clothing is removed. That is why it is important to also pay attention to a change in attitude or signs of depression in a teenager, such as ignoring personal hygiene, losing or gaining weight, and appearing to be suffering from a lack of adequate rest or sleeping too much.

Those who experience or witness physical abuse at home typically suffer from feelings of diminished self-esteem and self-worth, shame, and isolation. They often deny the problem and blame themselves for what happens. During adolescence, these children develop a higher risk for chemical dependency, extreme codependency in interactions with peers, depression, lack of motivation, even suicidal thoughts and actions.

Sexual Abuse

Any sexual act between an adult and a minor is considered sexual abuse. It also can occur between minors, such as siblings or schoolmates. Sexual abuse includes fondling, penetration, intercourse, exploitation, pornography, exhibitionism, child prostitution, group sex, oral sex, or forced watching of sexual acts.

Studies indicate that sexual abuse may be the most difficult for a teen to report because of feelings of deep shame, a sense of betrayal, and fears about the impact of such a report on the family. Any form of abuse experienced as a child or an adolescent has devastating consequences to the individual, the family, and, ultimately, to society.

Some symptoms of sexual abuse include depression, suicidal thoughts and attempts at suicide, self-inflicted injury, running away, homelessness, and eating disorders such as anorexia, bulimia, or compulsive eating.

The Effects of Sexual Abuse

Research findings link physical and sexual abuse of girls with subsequent substance abuse, poor academic performance, and early onset of sexual activity, which opens the door to a host of other problems: contracting sexually transmitted diseases (STDs), teen pregnancy, and sexual exploitation. There is also an increased risk for abused teens to become involved with the juvenile justice system. Boys who experience sexual abuse demonstrate excessive risk-taking behaviors, difficulties in school, aggressive and criminal behaviors, suicidal tendencies, and substance abuse.

Students who reported both physical and sexual abuse showed the highest rates of substance use. Abuse victims initiated substance use at a younger age than nonabused peers and gave more reasons for using, including coping with painful emotions and escaping from problems.

Abusers come from all walks of life, all socioeconomic, religious, and ethnic groups. Rarely is a child abuser a stranger to the teen. Typically, a person closely related to the teen, such as a parent, stepparent, or other family member or caregiver in the home, behaves abusively out of frustration and a feeling of being trapped in a stressful life situation with which he or she is unable to cope.

15

Your First Relationships: Home Sweet Home?

Every new life begins in love and hope. In the innocence of infancy, your life was sweet with possibilities. Now that you are a teenager, it still is. During adolescence, the way you interact with your family and friends is changing, like everything else in your life. It is important to understand the impact of your first relationships within your family. Before you can remember, before being influenced by peers, teachers, coaches, fashion trends, music, and Web sites, your behaviors, preferences, and anxieties were shaped by your family.

Your parents impart many gifts to you—some you appreciate more than others. Physical traits, like eye color, stature, and skin tone, are clearly visible. Other attributes, such as values, self-image, talents, and fears, may not be apparent initially. They can be likened to seeds planted underground, growing unseen within you until they emerge as parts of your personality. Your family's influence is a fact that cannot be extracted from your life, but it does not determine your destiny. It neither limits nor guarantees your own life goals.

Examining your past is a way for you to clear away some of the confusion that may be clouding the hope on your own horizon. Events that may have occurred with or without your conscious memory can trigger baffling responses in your life today. Looking back at what did or did not happen between you and your family members will help you understand how you got where you are now and why you may react to certain situations and people the way you do. It is about bringing to light secrets you may have been harboring that can lead to feelings of guilt, unworthiness, and a destructive thinking pattern known as denial (pretending to yourself and others that an unacceptable situation does not exist or is "not that bad").

Early Years

Studies show that a critical phase of brain development occurs in the first three years of life and can be adversely affected by improper nutrition, inadequate hygiene, limited access to medical care, and lack of attentiveness and other parenting skills.

On the other hand, children who are nurtured by loving, supportive parents in a stable home environment during these crucial years tend to get along better with peers, have a more comfortable rapport with authority figures, and achieve higher academic objectives. They have an increased chance of enjoying healthy relationships with peers at every stage of development.

In homes where parents regularly read to children and give them focused attention, children score higher on readiness tests when starting school. They are better prepared psychologically to venture out into the world, and they have a better chance of enjoying healthy relationships later in life. A stable home in which family members are treated respectfully is not the reality in every household, unfortunately. Teens who witness and/or experience disrespectful interactions in their own family tend to consider abusive habits normal behavior.

Parental decisions vary significantly regarding nutrition, discipline, and comforts needed in the family. Many parents apply, consciously or not, the same methods they recall from their own family dynamic, reenacting their parents' behaviors when rearing their own children. It is important to keep in mind that your parents' choices are based on the knowledge and capabilities available to them at the time, and most are motivated by love.

From your family members you first learn to ask for what you want, and you react to their responses. If you grew up in a busy home with lots of people and activities, you may have felt you were lost in the shuffle until you started to scream and cry. If others paid attention to you when you yelled, you learned a behavior that got results. As a teen, you may still associate being loud with having your needs met, without remembering where the habit originated.

Before developing their own abilities to decide what is appropriate, healthy, or effective, children and teens tend to model their behavior on their interactions with family members. Abusive cycles are perpetuated, unknowingly. Parents respond as they were responded to, believing their actions are justified and, possibly, in the best interests of the family.

"When I was growing up and my mother started screaming, I never knew what was wrong. I just wanted it to stop," says Madelyn, eighteen years of age and the mother of a two-year-old daughter. *"As a little child, I was terrified; as a teenager I was mad at her. She criticized me constantly. Nothing I did was ever good enough. I decided that when I had kids, I would never raise my voice or discourage them with put-downs.*

"But now, I sometimes realize I'm making sarcastic or mean comments to my daughter, and when I get frustrated, I start yelling. It's like I can't help it. It just slips out of my mouth. One day I sat down while my little girl was napping and I realized I was doing the same thing my mother did to me. I felt so bad, like I was a terrible mother, and I always thought it would just come naturally to me to be a good mom."

When Madelyn realized she was mimicking one of her mother's hurtful behaviors, she felt deep remorse, guilt, and a sense of failure. She did not know how to stop the behavior. Nor did she recognize it as emotional abuse.

Neglect

The most frequently reported child abuse in this country is child neglect. Child neglect is the failure to provide for basic needs, such as food, water, appropriate clothing, and safe shelter. Neglect can be physical, emotional, or educational. The Child Abuse Prevention and Treatment

Act (CAPTA) defines child abuse and neglect as any recent act or failure to act resulting in imminent risk of serious physical or emotional harm, death, sexual abuse, or exploitation of a child (a person under the age of eighteen).

Childhelp USA offers another definition to help recognize various forms of domestic abuse that affect teens: any commission or omission that endangers or impairs a child's physical or emotional health and development. Abuse includes damage done that cannot be explained reasonably, often an injury or series of injuries appearing to be nonaccidental in nature.

Examples of physical neglect include inadequate supervision, abandonment, expulsion from the home, or refusing to allow a runaway teen to return home. A refusal or delay in seeking medical care when it is needed is also a form of physical neglect. However, when evaluating a parent's failure to provide life necessities to a child or teen, it is important to bear in mind that some neglect issues are associated with poverty rather than the harmful intent of the parent(s).

Emotional neglect is a type of abandonment that is mental rather than physical. Marked inattention to a child's needs for affection or a teen's needs for emotional support is known to adversely impact the development of emotional, social, physical, and intellectual well-being. Behaviors classified as emotional neglect include ignoring, withdrawal of affection, and absence of positive reinforcement.

Counselors working with teenage drug abusers advise parents to praise any positive behavior demonstrated by the teen. Even when he or she is in trouble again, find something to praise; acknowledge that he or she is trying. The result of neglecting to offer positive reinforcement is a teenager who quits trying and gives up on life, escaping into self-destructive behaviors such as alcohol and drug abuse, and perhaps even suicide attempts.

Allowing a child of any age to witness spouse abuse and granting a minor (someone under eighteen years of age) permission to use alcohol or drugs are also considered emotional neglect.

Educational neglect includes allowing chronic truancy and failing to attend to a special educational need the child may have. Very often more than one type of neglect is occurring, and the ramifications tend to overlap.

What to Do When Home Makes You Hurt

The teen years can be a tough transition for the whole family. Your parents may know intellectually that they need to accept you for the person you are as you become an independent young adult. However, they may feel a sense of loss about the "sweet little child" they remember your being at age three, for example. In some cases, parents fear letting go of the control they had over you and your activities when you were younger. Often, your need to spend time with your friends and be apart from the family worries your parents, and they may place restrictions on your social time that seem unreasonable and unnecessary to you.

Parents often become frustrated, hurt, and angry about the same changes in you that you think are so cool: provocative clothing, wild hair styles, lax attitude toward school work, and new friends. You are turning a corner in your development; you seem to need your parents less. Both you and your parents may feel inadequate, unable to please each other anymore. Parents complain that you don't appreciate what they do for you; teens rebel against too much pressure to conform, be responsible, improve academic achievement, find a part-time job, or think about college. Tensions mount, and the gap between you and your parents widens.

A common concern cited by parents is the failure of discipline methods that sufficed in younger years. When adolescents appear unresponsive and unaffected by parental authority, parents often react out of fear and a sense of helplessness. They are especially apprehensive when they disapprove of the choices their teen is making, and they may feel a need to increase the severity of disciplinary actions in an effort to regain control.

Typical topics of conflict between parents and teens include disputes over the teen's:

⮑ Choice of friends

⮑ Curfew

⮑ School and work performance

⮑ Clothing, hair styles, makeup, body piercing, tattoos

⮑ Car and driving privileges

⮑ Telephone time

⮑ Household responsibilities

⮑ Dating and sexual behaviors

⮑ Spending time with family versus peers

⮑ Experimentation with smoking, drinking, and drugs

Meanwhile, this age is no picnic for you, either. It may seem that no one, least of all your parents, understands the pressure you feel. Peers, parents, teachers, coaches, and "significant others" who may be casual dates or intimate partners all make demands on you. Magazines, television, and other media images hold up idealized standards that are impossible for the average person of any age to attain.

Confusion All Around

Being a teenager is tough. You have to deal with sudden physical changes brought on by hormones and growth spurts. Your mind is filled with the drive to find your place, fit in, and be popular. Your heart aches for the attention of someone in one of your classes who seems to be unaware of your existence. You're expected to keep up with schoolwork while possibly juggling a job and your social life.

Trying to house all these internal forces, you may feel anxious, confused, fearful, angry, and alone. Teenagers from a full range of home environments struggle to get comfortable with their own identity while considering complex social issues: dating, sexual interests, school fights, drinking, and drug use. This process is further complicated for teens trying to cope with (and keep secret) the shame of emotional, physical, or sexual abuse at home.

Teen hotlines have been set up in many areas, and they are staffed by counselors who are trained to let the teen vent and at the same time determine the teen's immediate needs. Assessments and actions taken are based on each individual phone call. The counselor may just listen and refer the teen for counseling and appropriate support programs. If the counselor determines that the teen is in immediate danger of self-harm or being hurt by others, emergency services are notified. The call for help and support could be a new beginning for a teen in trouble with an abusive relationship at home.

If you notice that your friend has visible signs of physical abuse, like bruises that don't seem to have a reasonable explanation, talk to him or her. Let your friend know you are not just being nosy—that you care. Listen without judgment or showing any overreaction to what your friend tells you. Then encourage your friend to tell an adult or perhaps you can go to your parents together, if that is comfortable for you both.

If you are the one who is being hurt at home, you may be an expert at using makeup, long-sleeved shirts, or baggy clothing to hide a black eye, swollen lip, or bruised arms. You may create excuses for the injuries you cannot conceal. Hiding the evidence to protect the family member who supports you financially seems to be part of your survival. In reality, abuse does not improve with time; it gets worse. Keeping the secret also hides the need—and chance—to get help.

What You Can Do to Help at Home

Sometimes it is difficult to talk to your parents when you are feeling confused, hurt, or angry. But it is critical to try to keep communication open. It is a good idea to choose a time to broach topics of concern when the environment is calm and family members are relaxed—not rushing off to work or school and not when anyone has been drinking. Parents are more likely to be receptive at times when they are not stressed.

Some families find it helpful to have something written down in a contract format. Family members can discuss the contents of the agreement, sign the finished document and refer to it when conflicts arise over responsibilities, rules, and behaviors.

Rules such as, "Family members will not put down or insult each other, use vulgar or demeaning language, either privately or in front of others," should appear in the contract. Making a commitment among all family members to practice this rule could go a long way to ease tensions in a verbally abusive household. Typically, if the disagreement can remain respectful in the verbal phase, the situation is less likely to escalate to physical abuse. The contract will help prevent the breakdown of respectful communication.

The contract should provide clear-cut agreements on issues such as curfew, communications, privacy, conflict resolution, privileges, allowance, and household responsibilities. Fair and appropriate consequences should be delineated for those times when responsibilities are not upheld. In this way, every individual in the household is accountable for his or her actions (or refusal to act in accordance with the contract). An example of a teen/parent contract can be found on the Internet at www.help4teens.com.

While some disagreements and heated arguments inevitably accompany a teen's journey over the bridge to becoming an adult, the warning signs listed in this book indicate a dangerous intrusion past appropriate boundaries. If your parent is resorting to physical violence in an attempt to "get through" to you, the situation has pushed past the point of discipline, becoming abusive. Threats, throwing objects, shoving, and other aggressive

"Never Again"

Researchers document a cycle of violence, a three-stage pattern in what occurs before, during, and after a violent attack. Stage I is called the "Tension-Building" phase. The abuser may appear edgy, moody, agitated, and unpredictable. The victim proceeds cautiously, "walking on eggshells" in the abuser's presence, sensing danger. Learn to recognize if there are any patterns in your abuser's behavior indicating an impending attack, and be ready to proceed with your personal safety plan when these conditions appear to be brewing.

Stage II is described as the "Acute or Abusive" stage. This is the most violent and dangerous stage when emotions seem to erupt like a volcano. Verbal abuse spews forth, perhaps followed by physical abuse. Sometime later—it could be minutes, hours, or days—Stage III, the "Honeymoon" phase, occurs.

In the Honeymoon phase, the perpetrator feels and expresses remorse, promising the violence will never happen again. This pattern is typical among abusers, whether parent, stepparent, or dating partner. The "love" expressed keeps the victim believing the abuse will end and the relationship will survive.

If you grew up on this merry-go-round of abuse and broken promises, it may seem normal by the time you reach adolescence. It is not. Behaving perfectly and staying out of the way will not prevent the attacks from recurring. Abuse victims of any age want the hitting and humiliation to end, not the relationship. They want to believe the abuser's promises. However, research confirms that the abuser does not stop the behavior without learning how to do so through counseling or other intervention.

behaviors by the teen or parent are signs that the relationship needs guidance to get back on course.

Although research conducted by many childcare experts indicates that physical punishment and verbal shaming are ineffective teaching tools and far more damaging than helpful to the development of a well-adjusted individual, these methods are still widely practiced in homes. This may be because of a lack of awareness, high stress, poor parenting skills, or parental disagreement with the experts' opinions. If you are being abused emotionally, physically, or sexually in your home, do not dismiss or excuse the incidents, or blame yourself for them. Everyone needs discipline, but nobody deserves abuse.

Programs That Help

Caring about your own safety and well-being does not mean you are betraying your parents. Getting help for the whole family may be your best chance for reconnecting with them. Further, when the parent is reacting to his or her own stress, physical discipline can easily be taken to dangerous extremes. And as you grow older, bigger, and stronger, your retaliation becomes more likely—and more dangerous.

"My mother woke me up screaming at me, and she wouldn't stop," seventeen-year-old Cassandra tells her support group. "Then she punched me, and I shoved her to get her out of my face. I had a hangover, and I wasn't going to take that. She called the police. Juvenile court sent me here. My mother is getting counseling, too."

Domestic violence prevention classes may be recommended for all family members, or ordered by the court system once a police report is made. Many local organizations and crisis shelters provide such classes. They have proven effective for family members who keep an open mind and try to implement at home the tools learned at these programs. It often takes time to learn to practice a new way of living together as a family. In many cases, the situation improves when family members participate in specific classes, group therapy, community support groups, and individual counseling sessions.

Montrae M. Waiters, BS, Lead Juvenile Case Coordinator for The Spring of Tampa Bay, developed and facilitates a juvenile domestic violence intervention program called Peace in Action. The twenty-three-week curriculum emphasizes self-respect and respect for others, and involves the discussion of various topics, including "Alternatives to Violence," "Dating Violence," "Self-Esteem," "Communication," "Positive Choices," and "Setting Goals."

"I know this program has an impact," attests Ms. Waiters. "I see family dynamics improving, teens making better grades in school, finding the courage to leave bad relationships, and working to build a better life after participating in these classes.

"Self-respect and respect for others is key in helping these teens and families interact peacefully. I emphasize the importance of showing respect so others will be willing to help you out when you need it, not shut down on you."

"I find, in many cases, parents have not enforced boundaries and consequences when their children were young.

Then, suddenly, when the kids reach adolescence and crave independence, parents start trying to exert all this control, which causes clashes. We ask for all parents to come to class with their teen every fourth class in the month. The ones who do attend make great strides in practicing peaceful conflict resolution and getting along better with their teens."

If family interactions do not improve after trying counseling, parenting classes, and other supportive measures, CPS may intervene to remove the teen from the home temporarily for a cooling-off period while further evaluations continue. This is not a step that is taken lightly or without good cause. It is done to provide safety and protection, and it is not needed in all cases.

What Happens When a Call For Help Is Made?

If you think you are being abused at home, report it. Let the experts investigate. When the abuser attacks you in your home, the following steps are recommended.

⇝ Go to a different part of the house, away from the abuser. If possible, go into a room with a door that will lock. (Sometimes locks are removed or broken in homes where abuse occurs.) If you cannot detach physically from the abuser, drop to the floor and curl up in a ball to protect vital areas of your face and body.

⇝ As soon as you can safely do so, get out of the house and go to a neighbor's or friend's home or somewhere else that is safe.

↪ Place a call to the police or a child abuse hotline. Do not return home. Wait there until you are advised of the next step.

↪ A call to the police or a child abuse hotline results in a police report. This documentation may be needed for evidence in later court proceedings.

↪ A police officer and someone from the Department of Children and Families comes to your home to interview you, any nonoffending witnesses, and the offending parent or other perpetrator. If danger is immediate, authorities come to your family's home right away. Every action is decided on an individual, case-by-case basis. Laws vary significantly from state to state and are applied according to the type of injury discovered.

↪ In many areas, it is mandated that a home in which child abuse has been reported be evaluated within twenty-four hours.

↪ The information that comes from the personal interviews will determine the next step.

↪ The perpetrator might be arrested, and the teen may be removed from the home immediately.

↪ Social workers try to find a relative or family friend who will allow the teenager to stay in his or her home. This may be a temporary arrangement.

↪ If the nonoffending parent is able to protect the child or teen, the victim will not be removed from the home. Unfortunately, it is not always possible for the nonoffending parent to guarantee that degree of protection.

➥ The State Attorney's office is responsible for determining if a crime has been committed and for pressing charges against the perpetrator.

➥ Family counseling, parenting classes, and anger management courses may be ordered by the court system.

➥ If the parent (or perpetrator) is being cooperative and the situation shows signs of improvement, the teen may be returned to the home. It depends upon the dynamics in each individual family. One call for help does not necessarily mean the teen will be placed in foster care.

➥ Anybody who works with children is a mandated reporter. That means a school nurse, teacher, or counselor must report signs of child abuse upon becoming aware of it. If you tell a trusted adult or friend what is happening, that person will likely place the call for you. Even if you feel a strong bond with the nonoffending parent and want to protect your family, this call will ultimately help, not hurt, you.

Although you cannot know exactly what the outcome will be when you make a call for help with an abusive relationship in your home, making that call is your best chance to stay safe. You also do not know how much more dangerous your situation may become without intervention. Because it progresses, child abuse—even for a teen—is not just painful and humiliating; it can be fatal. It is too much for you to handle on your own. The move to foster care may become permanent in extreme family situations. However, every effort is made to improve the situation, remove the problems, and keep the family intact. The shared goal is a home that is a safe, healthy, and nurturing environment for all family members.

Hiding Out

If you live in a home torn by abuse of any kind, you may have devised your own survival mechanisms, such as staying at your friends' homes and never inviting them to yours. It is a temporary solution; eventually you must go home. Meanwhile, parents may feel they are left in the dark about who you are with and what interests you are sharing. This raises the level of discomfort parents already feel about your "mysterious" friends and what you are "up to" when away from home.

On the other hand, if you are afraid your parents will disapprove of your friends, consider that a "red flag" about the friends you are selecting. Are you choosing wisely and with your own best interests in mind? Or are you hanging out with whoever is available so you can stay away from home? Falling into the wrong crowd is easy to do at this age and in this circumstance. You may be replacing one difficult situation with another that is even more dangerous.

Break the Silence

There has been some documentation regarding teenagers' reluctance to report abuse for a variety of reasons. Teens who are establishing their independence from adults prefer to handle situations for themselves if possible. Some teens find it difficult to confide in an adult.

Studies indicate that abused girls and boys often kept the abuse a secret. When asked about reporting their abuse, 29 percent of girls who had been sexually or physically abused said they had not told anyone about the incident(s). Girls who had talked to anyone about abuse were most likely to confide in their best friend (41 percent) or their mother (38 percent).

Abused boys were even less likely to discuss their experience of physical or sexual abuse with someone: about half (48 percent) said they had not told anyone. When abused boys did talk to someone, their primary confidantes (29 percent) were their mothers. The desire for self-sufficiency is admirable and a natural aspect of being a teenager, but it is mature and courageous to ask for help.

"Silence is violence. If we can talk about it, we can change it." This statement is part of the philosophy of an organization that makes available a full spectrum of resources for teens through a middle- and high-school-based curriculum focused on preventing teen abuse. A branch of the Los Angeles Commission on Assaults Against Women (LACAAW), has devised a youth violence prevention program called Project TAP (Teen Abuse Prevention). The Commission's Web site can be accessed at www.lacaaw.org/prevention/tap.

Project TAP's comprehensive eight-unit curriculum, In Touch with Teens, addresses the causes of violence and the prevention of domestic violence, dating violence, rape, and sexual harassment. Project TAP programs have been distributed nationally and internationally for use in middle and high school settings. This group provides teens with information and skills needed to prevent and recover from abusive situations at home, school, and while dating. Its domestic abuse prevention curriculum offers training workshops, skits, and crisis intervention for youth, using telephone hotlines, in-person counseling, and small teen support groups at high schools. It is just one example of many innovative educational outreach and prevention programs now being funded and used across the nation.

This and other teen abuse prevention programs across the country emphasize the importance of not keeping abuse a secret. In an abusive home environment, it is part of the family dynamic to instill in the children a sense that it would be a betrayal to reveal secrets to the outside world. This indoctrination makes it more difficult to report abuse. However difficult, you can do it; and others will help you through it. Letting someone know when you are being hurt at home is the only chance for you and your family to heal. If you have been threatened or assaulted (physically or sexually) or if you feel you are not safe in your home at any time, there are two things you can do to get immediate help: tell a friend or make a call to report the abuse to a crisis hotline.

The National Domestic Violence Hotline, at (800) 799-SAFE (7233), offers support and local referrals. State and local 800 numbers for this same organization in your area are listed in your telephone book. The organization responds to thousands of calls each month. Support is available in English or Spanish, twenty-four hours a day, seven days a week.

If you believe the abuse at home is related to drug or alcohol use by your parent(s) or legal guardian(s), ask a school guidance counselor about an in-school Alateen meeting, or call your local Alateen telephone number to find out about a meeting you can attend. Alateen is a support group composed of other teenagers living with alcoholic parents. The comfort provided in Alateen meetings is invaluable for any teen struggling to manage alcoholism in the family. The teen should attend Alateen meetings in addition to other counseling that may be recommended. The phone number is normally listed in front of the telephone book with other crisis lines and emergency contacts. Alcoholism and drug addiction are often accompanied by a full gamut of domestic abuse.

Making that first phone call for help can seem like the hardest thing in life to do. It is a tough choice for a teen, or anyone, to make. Deciding to value yourself enough to speak up is the first step on the path to recovering the life you deserve.

Safety Plan

Being prepared for whatever action you decide to take can make a huge difference in your safety. You can make a safety plan and adapt it to suit your needs. You should tell someone you trust about the abuse and devise a code word or phrase you can communicate secretly when you need help. Making the plan will motivate you to write down a list of people, agencies, shelters, hotlines, and other services you may need. Knowing how to contact and get to local agencies and shelters before you leave home is vital. Some shelters do not accept teens unless accompanied by a parent, with the exception of emancipated minors (teens who are working and living independently of their parents).

Compile information for your safety plan when your environment is calm; don't wait until your escape is urgent and you are upset, injured, and confused. If you need to get out of the house, have a plan, get support, and be careful. An example of a teen safety plan appears on the Web at www.safenetwork.net/teens/safety.html.

The action plan for teens coping with abusive relationships at home is twofold. First, understand that the abuse is not your fault; it is the abuser's problem and he or she needs help. Second, seeking support for yourself will help you feel better. Help in many forms is available, but you must speak up. Don't be afraid that letting go of your secret may change your life and the lives of your family members; change is part of growing and healing. Tell a trusted friend what is happening in your home.

More assistance is available today than ever before for teens trying to cope with abusive relationships. The hope for recovering from the pervasive effects of criminal behaviors such as raging, bullying, battering, stalking, and dating violence hinges on recognizing these acts and believing you deserve better treatment. There are confidential resources available to you online, by telephone, in library books, and from school guidance counselors. There are also local, state, and national crisis telephone hotlines and shelters for those who need immediate help or referrals. Today, there is much more awareness of the scope of these sensitive issues and a vast willingness to help those who need it. There is no reason to suffer in silence. Until you speak up, the abusive situation will not change.

Dealing with Peers

As you navigate adolescence, asserting your independence from your parents and spending more time with your friends, you cannot discount the effects of your family's relationship patterns. Nor can you keep familial patterns from surfacing in your friendships, dating experiences, and other relationships with peers.

In a volatile home where tempers flare without warning, you may have witnessed violent and disrespectful behaviors, which you first feared, then imitated in some cases. You may also have learned to stay out of the line of fire by keeping quiet and, perhaps, masking your feelings. You may not be comfortable expressing yourself openly and honestly, because throughout your childhood you were discouraged from doing that. If you were not allowed to have a voice at home, it can be a new and somewhat startling adventure to find your own voice with your peers.

The coping mechanisms that helped you survive an intimidating home environment may sabotage your efforts to make new friends, get close to people, and speak up for yourself. Trained from birth not to impose on others, you may adopt an unassuming demeanor that is perceived by peers as shy, unfriendly, secretive, or slow-witted. You may have learned at home that it is safer not to ask for what you really want as a means of adapting to repeated disappointments and broken promises. It may be difficult for you to take the necessary risks to build relationships, strive for goals, and live fully. It may be more familiar to hear negative messages that have become internalized self-talk: "No. I don't deserve that." "I'm a loser." You can hush that nay-saying voice inside your mind by boosting your self-esteem.

Growing up with a steady diet of uncertainty in an abusive home can lead to diminished self-esteem and trust, and can hinder your ability to share your ideas, humor, and concerns with others—even in a simple conversation. You may be afraid that if you let people really get to know you, they will decide you are not worthy of their friendship. If you have grown up with rough treatment at home, you may expect the same from your peers. You also may assume that it is okay to treat others abusively because it is all you know. Once you recognize them, however, you can modify behaviors that do not serve you well.

Although you cannot force other people to change their habits and behaviors, you certainly can alter your reactions to them, and stop worrying about what you presume peers are thinking about you. It is your own self-conscious attitude that fuels your imaginings of worst-case scenarios when interacting with others.

Managing Your Stress

Studies show evidence that long-term emotional problems such as depression, low self-esteem, suicidal thoughts, and suicide attempts are associated with child abuse and domestic violence. For this reason, studies have been conducted to discover how teenage boys and girls cope with emotional stress. According to the Commonwealth Fund Survey of the Health of Adolescent Boys, generally, boys and girls tried different means to manage emotional stress. Boys were more likely to deal with their stress by exercising or using computers. Girls were more likely to talk to friends. Some 44 percent of boys said they called their friends when stressed, compared with 70 percent of girls.

Encouraging males to open up more verbally, rather than sulking silently, is one step psychologists are taking to better understand and help prevent the repressed anger that fuels the devastating violence in homes and in our society.

Community groups like Men Overcoming Violence (MOVE) strive to offer a better sense of emotional balance to adolescent boys, men, and their families. MOVE has developed comprehensive programs in violence prevention, educational outreach, counseling, and support for men who have been abused and for those who are seeking help to stop abusing. There are many such programs from which teenage girls and boys can draw supportive ideas for breaking the cycle of abuse.

A participant in a violence prevention program for teens, Joe, age sixteen, shares his story:

> "I wasn't thinking of anything when I pulled out the knife, except I was going to shut him up," says Joe. "The guy's always insulting my mother, man, and calling me names like 'Chico.' I hate being called that. I just get so mad, I can't think. He backed off, though, when he saw the knife. I never touched him. He called the cops. Now I'm under house arrest."

The counselor pointed out the possible conse-quences if the fight had turned out differently. Then he asked Joe to talk about why he felt so angry. Other teens in the group volunteered to discuss anger man-agement tools that had worked for them. Taking a deep breath and thinking a positive thought about yourself before speaking or reacting was recommended by one of the other teens. Someone else said, "Take a walk," to remove yourself physically from the verbal abuse and insults. Another said, "Remember the consequences—jail ain't no fun."

Changing Your Thinking

When you alter your thought patterns from "stinking thinking" to positive, constructive ideas about yourself, you relate better to others. And it is less likely others will be able to hurt you. For example, when someone snubs you at school or a social event, instead of thinking "Why me? What did I do to deserve this?" consider "Do I have a part in this or is it 'just one of those days' for the other person?" Ask yourself if there is anything you can learn from the experience. If so, try to learn and consider the experience a lesson, or a learning experience. If not, let it go. Forget about it. Know that you are fine, whether someone else thinks so or not.

Remember that "people pleasing" is a codependent behavior that is one of the effects of growing up in an abu-sive home. Thus, you may wish it were possible to make everyone your friend, but that is not a realistic expectation of yourself or others.

"I never fit in anywhere at middle school," confides Katie, age sixteen. *"I was put in special classes because of a learning disability. That was humiliating to me because I knew I was not stupid, but that's the label I got from other kids in the regular classes. Every day at lunch I sat with the same two friends. I had no other friends there. Most of the kids were rich and snobby. I felt like I was invisible.*

"My mother kept bugging me to take dance lessons so I finally tried it. When I was dancing, I had to really concentrate on every movement; I didn't think about what was cool or who was popular—or anything else except what I was trying to do. Turns out I really like dancing, and I made some friends at the studio.

"Two years later, I auditioned for a performing arts high school. I was accepted to the dance program. My best friends are dancers, and my boyfriend is in the theater program. I graduate this year and plan to start junior college in the fall. I'm glad I found dance—something I am good at that I like doing. Once I did that, it was easier to make friends."

Self-Acceptance

To help their clients believe they deserve love and respect from peers, many therapists recommend "mirror work." Looking into a mirror and telling your reflection "I love you" may seem silly at first, and some people laugh through their initial attempts to do the exercise. However, the technique is intended to help bring about a number of realizations. Perhaps the primary one is that you must first love yourself before you are capable of giving and receiving love. It is hard to love yourself if the love you experienced at home got all mixed up with abusive behaviors that hurt you. Learning to relax and feel comfortable in your own skin allows you to enjoy being yourself, and others become more interested in making friends with you.

Mirror work is just one example of many processes available to you on your path of self-acceptance, self-love, and self-respect. Improving your sense of self-worth begins with developing an awareness of what your values are—what is important to you to have in your life. Part of that is determining what is and is not acceptable behavior among peer groups. The next step is accepting the need for change if that is appropriate. The third is summoning your inner strength to take action.

Boundaries

Sometimes, no matter how much you work on your self-confidence, others continue to snub or harass you. In some cases, the abuser may notice a shift in the patterns of how you react to being provoked once you begin to build your self-esteem.

Sometimes the abuser steps up the taunting when your reactions change, so the abuse gets worse before it improves. That does not mean your plan has failed; it may just need more time. When you are new at trying to distinguish between healthy and abusive behaviors, the lines may become blurred. It is important to clarify your boundaries within yourself. For example, "I do not want to do drugs, shoplift, or spread rumors about other kids even if the popular kids are doing those things."

Helpful Hints

Listed below are things you can do to improve your relationships with peers by bringing to light the best of yourself.

- Don't be afraid to be yourself. Trying to be something you're not because you believe others think it's cool drains your energy and distracts your focus from your true goals. Misrepresenting yourself can also backfire horribly, catching you in a lie. Many teens are unsure of their self-image and enjoy trying different styles, peer groups, and interests. That's fine as long as you remain true to yourself in the process.

- Find others who share your goals. Decide what is important to you, and seek out others with similar interests and beliefs. For instance, if you are against using drugs, don't associate with those who are known to be experimenting with drugs and alcohol. If you like writing for the school newspaper or playing in the school band, get involved with those groups even if they are not the most popular ones.

- Respect others for who they are. Self-acceptance lays the foundation for accepting and getting along with others. If you have an opportunity to help someone else feel accepted into a group, step up and do it. The favor may be returned someday when you are feeling isolated and unsure. Pointing out the good in others helps others see your best qualities.

↪ If you feel as if you don't fit in, consider joining a club or extracurricular activity at your school, church, or community group. Choose something that interests you, rather than following the crowd. If the clubs at school don't work for you, look into some of the volunteering opportunities outside of school that may suit you better. Sharing similar interests opens the door to enriching and lasting friendships. If you don't know what your interests are, do a little more soul-searching. Check out something new; if it's not right for you, try something else and keep trying.

↪ Try to be a part of the solution, not the problem. Suggest alternatives or compromises if there is disagreement about where to go, what to do, or how to complete a group project. Participate actively. Don't sit back and let others make all the decisions and do all the work. Nor should you insist on doing it your way. Let your enthusiasm shine through everything you do.

↪ Most people feel shy sometimes, but don't always wait for someone else to talk to you first. Jump in and start a conversation with someone about anything you may have in common. Talking to someone is not a big commitment, and the more you practice, the easier it gets.

↪ Commend, rather than criticize, the achievements and efforts of others. Try smiling and offering help when appropriate.

☞ If someone is taunting or challenging you in some way, try to keep your voice calm and quiet, smile, make a joke, then walk away. Bullies target those who appear small, weak, or alone. "Safety in numbers" takes on new meaning around the lockers in school hallways. It is like an insurance plan to surround yourself with as many friends as possible and travel between classes in a pack. Walk tall and try not to look like a victim. This can be tough to do if you have been a victim in the past, but it is something you can learn.

☞ Know that you don't have to tackle all the changes you wish to make immediately, and you don't have to do it alone. Talk with a trusted peer or adult about any uncomfortable feelings you have about any relationships. Whether you are concerned with the way you are being treated or how you are treating others, discussing it opens the door to helpful insights and/or guidance to further assistance when appropriate.

You may be familiar with the saying, "You can't give away what you don't have." It is very true with respect to what you contribute to your friendships. If courteous, respectful relationships have not been modeled in your home, it is less likely you will know how to recognize or exhibit those desirable behaviors and avoid unhealthy ones. You may not always make wise choices when gravitating toward peer groups.

"Everybody in the group had to steal something from the store," recalls Jessica, age thirteen. "It was just part of fitting in. I don't know why, but if you didn't swipe something, you were out. Everybody made fun of you. I went along because it seemed harmless, but afterward I felt really bad.

"One of my friends got caught stealing some makeup. They took her into an office in the back of the store and called her parents and the police. She was crying and offering to pay for what she had stolen. They refused. After seeing what happened to her, it seemed silly to take chances like that.

"Finding a different group of friends seemed smarter than getting caught shoplifting. But it wasn't easy for me. For a while, the old group teased me in the halls at school. I just pretended to ignore them even though I was dying inside. Pretty soon they got tired of it and left me alone. I guess they found someone else to harass."

Some people have what others call a "broken picker," meaning they tend to pick people who are not good for them. This happens when choosing friends and dating partners, which will be explored in further detail later in this book. Improving yourself will boost your confidence and self-image, but you may still be attracted to people and situations that are not in your best interests. It may take time to change the "broken picker" habit, but it can be done. As you grow, your peer group will grow, too, offering more choices about friends and how you will spend your social time.

Go with Your Gut

Sometimes, the best signals are the intuitive ones felt in the gut when you observe or participate in a situation driven by peer pressure. A warning sign you may notice in a potentially abusive friendship is a serious power imbalance. The "leader" controls or tries to control you and the rest of the group. Insulting you when you don't go along with the crowd and pressuring you to do something you do not want to do are abusive behaviors that can lead to all kinds of trouble, including brushes with the law.

Learning to detach from an unhealthy friendship or peer group without worrying that you have ended your social life can be tough. It is an important skill to learn, both for self-preservation and more satisfying relationships. It is a self-care issue that is as critical as proper nutrition and adequate rest. Declaring your independence from a situation that is not healthy for you means you are taking care of yourself. It does not mean you do not care about the other person(s), although that accusation may be thrown at you.

You are not responsible for the choices of others. However, if you choose to hang with a group of people involved in unacceptable behaviors, such as drinking, using drugs, stealing, bullying, or cutting classes at school, you are responsible for your choices and actions. You are accountable for your participation and your silence about the offending activities. The consequences are real, and you alone will face them if you are caught.

"My boyfriend and all his friends were smoking pot," recalls Lauren, sixteen. *"I didn't really want it because I don't like smoking anything, but I felt like an idiot just passing on the joint every time it came around to me. Finally, I took a hit and had some kind of allergic reaction. I sneezed and sneezed; I couldn't stop. They all laughed at me; it became a big joke.*

"Secretly, I was glad I could say I was allergic and they never pressured me to try smoking pot again. But I got bored with them because all they wanted to do was sit around, get stoned, and do nothing. Eventually my boyfriend and I broke up. I felt lost at first and had to find a whole new group. Any time the question of smoking pot comes up, I just say I am allergic. As far as I'm concerned, that's the truth."

Walking away from a group or a dating relationship that is not good for you may result in some alone time until you find a new situation that suits you better. Exercising your choice to detach yourself is personally empowering, and the time you spend alone in the interim may be beneficial in the long run. Try to believe that a better friendship, a more satisfying romance, and a brighter world are just around the corner.

Empowering
Choices at School

Popularity is an elusive commodity, like a silver bead of mercury that slips through your fingers just when you think you have a grip on it. Friends come and go, sometimes leaving you feeling betrayed. Being "in" with the "in crowd" can be fun and empowering, yet painfully fleeting. The formula for being a popular teenager varies among schools and different peer groups, and the factors get switched unpredictably. Having a girlfriend or boyfriend typically contributes to your acceptance among peers at school.

In some middle and high schools, popularity is influenced by your family's affluence. In other schools, presenting a certain look may win you peer group acceptance. In some settings, it's cool to make good grades; in others, academic achievement marks you as a nerd.

In most schools, boys who do well in team sports have a better shot at fitting into the popular groups. Boys who are small or not talented in sports may flounder in search of an acceptable group and are more likely to be targeted for taunting, particularly in gym class. Coaches should be made aware of and take action against harassment and abusive behaviors occurring "on their watch" during gym class. These situations escalate quickly and can result in serious injuries, both physical and psychological. If the coach is unresponsive to complaints, a parent or school administrator should be notified.

Traditionally, girls have been more interested in cheerleading and supporting boys' games than in playing their own. Today, more teenage girls seize the opportunity to get into the sports, joining co-ed or girls' soccer, basketball, softball, and other team activities. These offer great benefits that girls need as much as boys: enhanced fitness, team-centered camaraderie, the drive to challenge their personal goals, the thrill of winning. Since most females are as likely as males to enter a competitive workplace and support a family today, the team sports experience, at its best, is valuable for both genders.

As previously mentioned, a teen may need to confide in a trusted adult at some time. That could be a coach, particularly if the coach models an encouraging attitude, good sportsmanship, and other positive behaviors. On the other hand, a coach may be crossing the line into abusive behaviors if he or she chides, chastises, and demands unreasonable physical feats under the guise of "conditioning" players on the team. Losing sight of the real needs of youth team sports and focusing only on winning may blur the boundaries of acceptable behavior among teammates and coaches.

Youngsters who are familiar with the shaming tactics of adults at home or school may not recognize their coaches' behavior as unacceptable. These teens are more likely to become discouraged by harsh criticisms and put-downs—deciding they are not "good enough."

The sports experience, then, chips away at self-esteem, rather than building it.

Who's In? Who's Out?

For many reasons, both girls and boys tend to feel most comfortable at school and social events when surrounded by their friends. How are these groups formed? What does it take for you to be welcomed into a group? What can really hurt your chances?

Children Without Friends, a study conducted by S.R. Asher and G. A. Williams, and sponsored by The National Network for Childcare (NNCC), lists common reasons for peer acceptance and rejection.

Traits others like and accept:

⇒ Is fun to be with

⇒ Can be trusted with a secret

⇒ Is a positive influence on others

⇒ Encourages others

⇒ Sticks up for friends

⇒ Shares common interests, beliefs, and goals

⇒ Helps friends achieve their goals

⇒ Listens well and is supportive

⇒ Has a great sense of humor, but not at others' expense

Traits others dislike and reject:

⮑ Is "too pushy," aggressive, and dominates others

⮑ Acts withdrawn, standoffish, uncaring, and seldom participates

⮑ Has "bad energy," or negative attitude, or is sarcastic

⮑ Interrupts conversations or does not listen to others

⮑ Lacks abilities in important peer activities like sports

⮑ Acts uncooperative, inconsiderate, not interested in helping peers

⮑ Insults others with put downs and name-calling

⮑ Betrays friends' confidences, gossips, starts rumors

⮑ Has a bad temper

⮑ Gets in trouble at school

Your peers initially respond to you based on how you appear to them, and they can only see what you let them see. If you are hiding a secret, like an abusive relationship at home or in a dating relationship, you are likely to guard how much you reveal about yourself to your peers. You may unintentionally project a false image of yourself or hold back aspects of your personality that are the most endearing to others.

This habit of keeping certain aspects of yourself hidden often results from an abusive home life that remains a secret under the code of silence practiced within the family. This is one way the effects of abusive family relationships carry over into relationships with peers. You may not even be aware you are projecting this mysterious or secretive image to others, but they may perceive you as "holding back" without knowing why. Trying to see yourself as others see you sometimes helps you find ways to be more open and confident among your peers.

Body Language

Going back to the mirror work, use your reflection now to observe yourself the way others see you. Notice your posture. Are your shoulders slumped and rounded as if trying to enclose your chest? Body language studies indicate that this stance is common among people who have been harshly criticized. What happens if you pull your shoulders back, opening your chest? Do you look different? How does it feel?

Observe the way you carry yourself and move across a room. Do you walk with confidence or cower as if walking on eggshells? Notice the way you dress. Do you unleash your own flair of individuality? Are your clothes antagonistic, with negative images or words on them? Do you wear fashions and brands that let you blend in with the way others dress? Do you wear only black? Is that your preference or someone else's? Consider the messages being sent by your appearance, before you ever even speak.

Sometimes the mirror—or your vision—plays tricks on you. It reveals an image that is distorted by a common

Eating Disorders

Individuals who develop eating disorders perceive their body image as "fat," regardless of how thin their reflection really is. Eating disorders such as anorexia and bulimia are more common in teenage girls than in boys, but both genders can be affected. The disorder often is triggered by an upset over a specific event: an unwanted break-up, the divorce or remarriage of parents, a move to a new school, being ousted from a group of friends. The obsession becomes the belief that "Nobody likes me because I am too fat" or "My body makes me miserable."

When your self-image is low, internalized fears warp your vision like the trick mirrors in a carnival fun house. You may see yourself as over-weight, ugly, awkward, and unlikable, though others may not perceive you that way at all. Low self-image can be cured, not by starving yourself, but by changing your thinking.

plight among teens known as "low self-image." You may find fault with your image and focus on any imperfections, exaggerating their impact. If you go to school believing that you will fail or that nobody likes you, the chances of that happening are increased. But if you go to school with a positive vision of yourself as capable, cooperative, and cool, you design for yourself a more encouraging prophecy to fulfill.

Confronting Issues

You may not always agree with the group's decision about a potential new friend. It is a courageous act to remain open-minded and honest about what is important to you, whether or not it is the popular opinion. It is even more courageous to speak up on behalf of someone who has been deemed "not cool" for whatever reason. Going against the crowd to stand up for a rejected peer can be risky. It may alienate others and cost you the comfort of your familiar peer group. For most teens, that risk is too great. Remaining silent while the dominant personalities speak for the whole group is the norm. This silence makes it even more difficult to turn the tide of the popular group's influence.

Even though it can be scary, expressing yourself in your relationships with peers helps develop communication skills you will use your whole life. Conflicts that arise at home, school, work, and in personal relationships often stem from poor communication and misunderstandings. If you feel angry, fearful, anxious, or especially nervous for some reason, you are more likely to get flustered, mis-speak, and not hear what is being said the way it was intended. If you let this fear keep you from confronting someone, the awkward silence grows and there's less chance for the situation to get better. Confronting the issue cannot guarantee the outcome you desire, but it allows you to move through the problem, which is liberating.

To confront a problem verbally, you should:

- Identify the problem. Know exactly what you are really upset about. Is it a betrayal of trust, an offending remark, a rumor, a snub?

- Focus on that issue—the problem—not the person. Do not blame the other person for what you feel, though it is appropriate to express what you feel.

- Try to understand the other person's point of view, even if you do not agree with it. Listen respectfully, ask questions to clarify as needed, and summarize what you believe the other person said. This helps clear the fog of confusing miscommunication.

- Respond by expressing your position and reasons, respecting your own boundaries and those of the other person.

- Work together to come up with a compromise or other options that both parties accept with some satisfaction.

- Decide together on a fair solution.

- Ask for help resolving a difficult conflict by using a peer mediator when necessary. A mediator may be a peer whom you both trust to be fair and not take sides. This objective person can help you both stay focused. School guidance counselors can assist in connecting you with a peer mediator at your school. It is a conflict resolution method that has proved successful in many schools.

To make your points during an argument, don't:

↝ Clench your fists, tighten your jaw, cross your arms, roll your eyes, shake your head, or display other body language that tells the other person you are not open to listening.

↝ Interrupt, criticize, put down, threaten, blame, tease, make excuses, change the subject, or laugh at the other person.

↝ Raise your voice or exhibit threatening gestures, such as throwing objects.

↝ Sulk in silence, feign indifference, or refuse to communicate at all.

If you have done all you can do to help resolve the problem and you still feel angry or uncomfortable with the other person, it may be time to step back to your separate corners and take a breather. Perhaps the two of you are not going to be friends; you can agree to be courteous and respectful and let each other be.

If an agreement to leave each other alone is not upheld and the other person persists in upsetting or threatening behaviors, further action may be needed. If you are the quick-witted "teaser" who initiates name-calling and can always come up with a sarcastic put-down, insult, or "joke" at the expense of others, check yourself. Think about the other person's personal boundaries, which you are invading with your words. If you were brought up in an abusive home, boundary invasion was probably a regular practice. Remind yourself that this behavior is not normal, not okay, and ultimately does not win friends.

Bullies

The Health of Adolescent Boys: Commonwealth Fund Survey indicated that overall, 16 percent of adolescent boys said they did not feel safe in their school or neighborhoods. Feeling unsafe in the classroom is certainly not conducive to learning, or even being able to concentrate on the lesson. Understanding possible sources of the violence in schools may help stop it.

Bullies put others down to make themselves appear more important in the eyes of their peers. If they were really confident individuals, they would not need to bully others. They target others they perceive as small, weak, or shy. They seek out someone who is alone, small and for some reason appears to be a victim. Or they may target someone out of jealousy or a dispute involving a girlfriend.

"For some reason, this one kid, Grant, decided I was not cool," says Alex, age thirteen. "He got this whole group of guys at school to call me 'loser' every time they saw me. They harassed me at my locker, kicking me and knocking books and papers out of my hands all over the floor, which sometimes made me late to class. I avoided going to my locker and just carried all my books around all day in my backpack. During some classes, they were real sneaky about it so they didn't get conduct cuts, but they whispered insulting things to me about my family, my clothes— anything and everything about me was wrong.

"I had some friends, but not as many as Grant, and everyone was afraid to stand up for me against that whole group. People said to just ignore it, so I tried, but this kid was wrecking my social life. He told other people not to invite me to their parties because he hated me. Grant and his friends told me if I showed up at any of the dances or hangouts where the popular kids go, they would all jump me.

"Finally, one day I was so mad I thought I would explode. I told my mother about it, and we talked for a while. She went to my school and talked to the guidance counselor, who then called me in and told me about peer mediation. But I wasn't interested in confronting Grant. I didn't believe it would work with him.

"Soon after that, I got to change schools, so now I never see Grant, though I run into some of his gang at the mall sometimes. When he's not around, there's no problem. I like my new school better. I am more popular there. Who knows why?"

Some dominant personalities at a school have a great deal of influence on their peers, and their victims may be left with few options. Alex was fortunate to be able to change schools, but bullies will likely confront him again. He will not always be able to change schools, so he should learn some coping skills and perhaps enroll in some form of self-defense program to boost his confidence and self-esteem.

How to Deal with Bullies

Tips for thwarting bullies include walking tall with your head held high to give the impression of confidence, even if you're faking it. A powerful-looking stance may discourage bullies from approaching you. Move about the school grounds with friends whenever possible. The slogan "safety in numbers" certainly applies to school halls and after school events.

Try to stay calm and ignore the bullies' taunting. Remember, they want a reaction, so don't give them one. Take a breath, think, then change the subject. You can say something funny or unexpected to confuse the bully and break the tension. Don't antagonize the bully, and never fight over any possessions. Do not fight at all if you can help it, but try not to look or act like a victim. Consider peer mediation and other options your school guidance counselor offers.

Here are some other things students can do to help keep peace at school:

- ❧ Refuse to bring a weapon to school, or carry a weapon for anyone else, and refuse to keep quiet about anyone who carries or discusses having access to weapons.

- ❧ Learn how to manage your anger and settle arguments by talking or walking away, rather than fighting.

- ❧ Start or join a peer mediation program to help others learn to settle disputes peacefully.

- ❧ Welcome new students and introduce them to others. Get to know someone new each week.

- ❧ Start or join a "peace pledge" campaign, in which students promise to settle disagreements without violence, reject weapons, and work toward a safe campus for all.

If you are being harassed by someone or a group of people, and they habitually taunt you or undermine you in front of other students, you need to recognize that there is a difference between "kidding around" and verbally abusive harassment. Verbal and emotional abuse challenge your right to feel safe at school and at after-school events. That is bullying, an important early link in the chain of violence.

If you have tried to handle the situation yourself and it is still not resolved, know when it is time to ask for help. Confide in a parent, teacher, or guidance counselor at school about the situation. They may not be aware of a problem unless you inform them. It is coming to light that school violence prevention needs to begin at the beginning—not with the weapon in the locker but with words, ideas, attitudes, and policies mandating the tolerance of differences and peaceful coexistence.

Dating Issues

Checking out classrooms for a boyfriend or girlfriend starts sooner than many parents realize. Experts say girls are fascinated with the notion of dating at an earlier age than boys, but this varies among individuals. As young as age nine or ten, many preteens are pushing the pedal to the metal, eager to become teenagers and start dating. By age twelve, most feel ready for romance. For teenage and preteen girls, having a boyfriend means attaining status among peers. A type of peer shaming often occurs when a girl has no boyfriend. Boys may feel a similar pressure to have girlfriends to demonstrate their masculinity. Carolyn, now age seventeen, remembers when the pressure to date began for her.

"When I was twelve, one of my best friends said to me: 'You're so cute. How come you never have a boyfriend?' From then on, I felt like I needed a boyfriend so everyone knew I was okay—and so I knew I was okay."

Having a significant other serves as a reassurance that a person is accepted. It may help a young girl believe she is attractive and lovable at times when her self-confidence wanes. This need for outside approval from males is magnified for a girl who has low self-esteem and/or concerns about her appearance. Teenage boys also feel they gain approval from their peers when they have a girlfriend.

In high school the pressure intensifies, as if time is running out, although it certainly is not. Teenage girls are less likely to focus on other interests and activities, such as sports, when they are worried about a boyfriend or why they don't have one. Girls are more likely than boys to think obsessively about their relationships and practice self-blame when anything goes wrong. When special events—like homecoming and prom night—loom on the horizon, a girl who is not going out with anyone particular may feel anxious about getting a date. She may decide not to attend the event unless she has a date, forcing herself to miss out.

For a boy, wanting to fit in with peers who are dating is a normal and harmless intention. However, the need to prove himself to peers "in the locker room" may result in a boy's trying to achieve "stud" status, bragging about his conquests and treating girls as objects to be possessed. This attitude can lead to unkind and disrespectful treatment of girls and, eventually, a sense of mistrust among peers of both genders.

This is not the type of person most girls want for a boyfriend. It may not be the type of person the boy really wants to be. He may think he has to play a role or he may be acting out a role he has seen modeled at home or in the movies.

Lighten Up!

Learning to lighten up and stop worrying about a relationship, or the fact that you may not be in one, adds a magical sparkle to your life. Accepting things as they are instead of fretting about why they are not as they "should be" will help you feel better and have more energy. In addition, you may find out that when you relieve yourself of the pressure to be in a relationship, you may attract more people to you effortlessly.

The people you attract when you are feeling positive are more likely to be the type of friends who will be good for you, rather than the type of people who might drag you down with negativity. Friends rally around a person who laughs, knows how to have a good time, and shares a positive outlook with others.

Group dating is a comfortable and common way to socialize. Going out on a date with a group of friends takes some of the pressure off one-on-one encounters, giving everyone in the group a chance to mix with friends of the opposite sex. But even within a group of friends, teens often hope to be part of a twosome they can count on.

Add to that the constant quest for popularity, which may be enhanced by dating the "right" person, and you may be left feeling a lot of pressure to connect with someone. In response to these pressing needs, some teens may forget or overlook the traits they need to develop and maintain a healthy relationship. They may be tempted to settle for someone who exhibits signs of abusive behaviors. There is a real cost in dating a person who promises love but shows signs of danger.

Warning Signs

You may be in an abusive relationship if your boyfriend or girlfriend exhibits the following behaviors. He or she:

- Is extremely jealous and possessive of you, demands all of your time, and seems to isolate you from others. (Jealousy is the primary symptom of abusive relationships.)

- Controls you by being demanding, bossy, coercive, or threatening.

- Loses his or her temper suddenly and violently.

- Abuses drugs or alcohol.

- Blames you for his or her emotional state. Also blames you when he or she mistreats you.

- Has a history of bad relationships.

- Makes "jokes" that belittle or embarrass you, both privately and among friends.

- Rages when feeling hurt, angry, ashamed, fearful, or out of control.

- Motivates your friends and family to warn you of their concern about the person and about your safety and well-being.

- Grew up witnessing an abusive parental relationship and/or was abused as a child.

⮞ Pressures you sexually, demanding sexual activities you feel uncomfortable doing.

⮞ Attempts to cope with pain through drug or alcohol abuse or dependence.

Relationships may become mutually abusive when a girlfriend or boyfriend who is being abused hits back or retaliates in other ways. The fact that both partners are abusive does not excuse the abuse or make the relationship healthy.

Without the help of counseling, self-help efforts, support from community or national organizations, or other outside intervention, a teen who has been abused at home will repeat abusive patterns observed and experienced in the family, choosing abusive (or potentially abusive) partners and friends. If you think you are in an abusive dating relationship, understand that you cannot make it better by doing exactly what the other person wants and being "perfect." The abuse will progress and will not end without intervention of some kind. Victims often say, "I know it will be different with me." Statistics disprove that fantasy.

Denial

Denial is a strong factor among abusers and their partners. It can be difficult to let go of a relationship even though you recognize that something is wrong. Studies show that the longer you wait to get out of a situation that is not right for you, the harder it becomes to find your strength and break free.

You may find it easier to justify your partner's extreme jealousy, for example. The self-talk that goes on in your head may sound something like this: "Well, I get jealous too—we love each other so much." You may also fool yourself with, "I hit him too, sometimes. We have a very passionate relationship." It is common for abusive behaviors to become mutual between partners. That does not make those behaviors acceptable. Another excuse for the inexcusable may be: "It only happens when he's been drinking," or, "I shouldn't have made him mad by being late, calling my friend, looking at another person, etc." You need to understand that you should not tolerate abuse of any kind. You have the power to end a relationship that isn't healthy.

Healthy or Unhealthy Relationship?

"Mike was my first serious boyfriend. We were in love and everything we did together was so much fun. He never told me not to see my friends, but he put them down, refused to hang out with them, and took up all my time. He got jealous and made a big scene once when he didn't know where I was for a few hours while I visited my best friend. My friends gave up calling me. I didn't feel right about that, but I figured it was a necessary compromise to keep peace in the relationship."

Isolating you from family and friends gives your partner more control over what you do, where you go, who you see, and how you live your life. Isolation can be accomplished in subtle ways or by overt commands.

The subtle tactics are more difficult to recognize. How do you know it's not just a love so strong you can't stand to be apart? Victims of domestic abuse are accustomed to isolation, so it may feel familiar, comfortable, and secure.

In a healthy relationship, partners encourage each other and support their achievements and goals. Do you feel encouraged to work toward your goals, even when they differ from your partner's? How do you feel about your partner's pursuing an interest that takes him or her away from you? If you were invited to go have dinner with a friend without your significant other, would that start an argument?

Extreme jealousy, peppered with angry scenes and wildly imaginative accusations, is not normal or healthy. It is the most common trait of an abusive partner. While most couples experience bouts of jealousy, the behavior is abusive when it becomes so extreme that the relationship feels like being held hostage. Avoid the person who thinks of you as a possession and tries to control the relationship and your life—no matter how charming he or she may be. Unpredictable mood swings, angry outbursts, and violent gestures—like smashing a fist into a door or throwing objects—are all indicators of an abusive and potentially unsafe relationship.

It can be tough to express what you are sensing, so it is critical for you to spend as much time as you need alone so you can examine your feelings about the relationship. If you have a bad feeling about a situation or a person, pay attention. Then get more information. Read, research, talk to someone you trust, and try to think for yourself.

Mutual Respect

Respecting another's beliefs even when they differ from your own can be challenging, but it is a mark of maturity. Allowing your partner to grow and develop fully as an individual is a sign of real love. It requires honesty and trust; it can be scary. The relationship may not survive, but if it stifles one or both partners, it is doomed anyway, although it may die a slower death.

Insisting on always having your way is not a sign of love; it is a sign of the need to maintain control in a relationship. Having the confidence to risk the relationship and reach out for your own chance at happiness comes from developing your self-esteem. Without that, it is difficult to take a stand and confront an issue that may cost you the relationship.

"He told me he went out with another girl because she would have sex with him. He wanted to see her again and still go out with me. I said we had to break up. I was in so much pain; I didn't know what to do to feel better, and I had no one to talk to. I thought all my friends were mad at me for dumping them.

"So I started going out with Mike again, agreeing that we could both go out with other people, even though I didn't want to. Again, the compromise didn't work for me. I just wanted things back the way they were when we first met."

It is natural for men and women to feel strong sexual desire for each other when they are in love, but acting upon that desire must be a mutual decision. Both partners must clearly consent and be prepared in advance with birth control.

71

Inside the Tornado

"Sex did not bring us closer; he still went out with other girls," says Carolyn. "I didn't trust him and was not interested in having sex with him again. A few weeks later, I told him I was afraid I might be pregnant. He said, 'No, it never happens the first time.' Sadly, he was wrong about that.

"By the time the test confirmed the pregnancy, Mike was starting college. He said we were too young to get married now; he would help me pay for an abortion. I never thought I would have to make that choice. It was like being caught inside a tornado: trapped and blown about in winds, powerless over what was happening to me. I felt like I wanted to die.

"Once more I agreed to do what Mike wanted to do instead of choosing what I wanted, which was to keep my baby. Again, I compromised to save the relationship.

"I want other girls to know what I had to learn the hard way. First, sacrificing yourself for a relationship does not work. Second, yes, you can get pregnant the very first time."

Carolyn never recognized her treatment as abusive until the consequences forced her to pay a dear price. She tried sacrificing herself in numerous ways to hold on to a failing relationship. She believed the relationship was more important than she was, which is a common fallacy. Carolyn was not able to say to her boyfriend, loudly, clearly, and repeatedly, "No!" She abandoned herself to save the relationship. Does it make sense to do that?

There is no magic formula for when it is appropriate to share in the joys of a loving sexual relationship, but it is essential that both partners agree the time is right.

Relationship Contract

You may want to consider making a relationship contract to help you understand what you want in your close relationships. Peace in Action, a program at The Spring of Tampa Bay, which encourages the prevention of teen violence, suggests that its participants complete a relationship contract. The contract should consist of questions that relate to dating, sexual rights, other relationships, and priorities. The purpose of this exercise is to help you figure out what your opinions are and whether or not you're compromising too much in your current relationship.

You should include questions such as: "How much time do I want to spend with my boy/girlfriend?" "When we go out, who decides what we'll be doing?" Other questions should relate to sex issues, such as: "Whose responsibility is birth control?" Questions about other relationships could include questions like "Does my partner get upset when I hang out with my friends?" And the last section should have questions about priorities: "What do you think is the most important quality that a boy/girlfriend should have?"

Answering these questions will help you realize what you're looking for in a relationship. You should settle for no less than what you truly want. There is surely someone out there that can meet your highest expectations.

When Love
Gets Dangerous

In the beginning, there are roses. Poems, love letters, kind words, long telephone calls, and thoughtful gifts contribute to the romantic spell. Thinking of your boyfriend or girlfriend fills you inside with a warm happiness. The problems of the world are like distant stars. Together the two of you feel complete, and life is perfect. So it was for Amaris, now fifteen years old, when she started dating a popular boy.

> "I started dating at twelve, although I was not allowed to date. I lied and sneaked out of my house to see him. He was a really cute, popular guy. For the first three months, it was great!"

An excellent resource on abusive dating relationships for teenagers is a book called *In Love & In Danger: A Teen's Guide to Breaking Free of Abusive Relationships* by Barrie Levy. Ms. Levy explores the serious nature of dating violence and defines three types of love: romantic, nurturing, and addictive.

The initial phase of most relationships is known as romantic love. It may last six weeks or six months, but it always changes. At some point after you both begin to see each other's faults, you feel the passion shifting. When you start giving the rest of your lives more attention, it does not mean the love has died or is not real. Love naturally evolves into a new phase, which the relationship may or may not survive. Many couples decide to break up when romantic love begins to change.

Partners in a nurturing love relationship encourage and support each other. The relationship is based on trust, not on fear of losing anything. People involved in a nurturing relationship feel safe even when they disagree, and they feel comfortable expressing themselves. Disagreements invite neither self-destructive feelings nor violent behaviors. Both partners strive for their individual goals; they grow without growing apart. They feel secure enough to allow each other this kind of freedom.

Addictive love functions more like a trap. Partners believe they cannot live without each other. One partner may express his or her need for the relationship with control, isolation, and criticism, convincing the other partner that nobody else will love him or her. He or she creates a sense of security for him or herself by making the partner feel totally dependent on the relationship.

Addictive relationships are at increased risk for becoming abusive. Individuals in addictive relationships will do anything, even exert force, to keep the relationship from ending or changing. Typically, partners ignore or make excuses for insults, inconsiderate or forced sexual relations, and battery (beating). Feelings of denial are strong in both perpetrators and victims. Partners may become mutually abusive, hitting back.

Heed Warning Signs

Recent national studies compiled by the Family Violence Prevention Fund indicate that overall, 36 percent of teens experience violence in their dating relationships. In a survey of 232 high school girls, 17.8 percent of the subjects indicated that they had been forced to engage in sexual activity against their will by a dating partner. The dangerously thin line between love and hate is demonstrated by this haunting statistic: One out of every three women murdered in this country is killed by her husband or boyfriend.

Victims of abuse at home are more likely to get involved in abusive relationships outside the home, but anyone can be in an abusive dating relationship. Dating violence occurs among teens and adults from all socioeconomic levels, in wealthy and impoverished neighborhoods. It happens in gay and straight relationships, in every culture and ethnic group.

A serious power imbalance, with the abuser in control, is a major warning sign for a future of abuse in a relationship or friendship. Here those warning signs are highlighted again with more detail pertinent to dating:

- ☞ Extreme jealousy and possessiveness is the primary symptom of an abusive relationship, not a healthy sign of love. It signals an insecure partner who will need constant proof of your love. The demands tend to become increasingly humiliating and dangerous.

- ☞ Controlling you by being demanding and bossy may be stepped up to subjecting you to demeaning sexual acts and total isolation from anyone or anything outside the relationship.

- His or her violent temper is set off suddenly and unpredictably, even when you "walk on eggshells" trying to keep the environment calm, peaceful, and happy—like it may have been in the beginning.

- Drug and alcohol abuse complicates everything in a relationship by adding layers of confusion. Relationships can be tricky enough without these added obstacles. Attempting to cope with life stress by using drugs and alcohol, and encouraging you to do the same, is damaging to any relationship.

- Blaming you for provoking your own maltreatment is common among abusers. It helps them assuage their feelings of guilt. Unfortunately, the guilt does not kick in until after the attack, and it vanishes again before the next attack. It is not a deterrent, but an afterthought. The abuser's blame reinforces the self-blame you already feel for not being perfect enough to keep him happy.

- History of bad relationships experienced by the abuser may be ignored if the victim thinks, "He is different with me." The apparent difference is temporary unless the abuser gets help to change his abusive behavior.

- The abuser makes "jokes" that belittle or embarrass you, both privately and among friends. Again, this practice gets "stepped up," with the comments often becoming more viciously critical. The abuser may tell friends intimate details or lies about your relationship purposely to embarrass you.

☞ Rage always reveals a loss of control and is not tolerable under any circumstances. Nobody has the right to get in your face and scream or scold or tell you you're no good. If your parents did it, it's still not acceptable for a girlfriend or boyfriend to do it.

☞ Friends' and family's warnings and concerns for your safety and well-being should be taken seriously. They are objective onlookers from outside the relationship, which can be a valuable and honest perspective. Their motives are loving. They may ask about things that are painful for you to reveal; that does not mean they want to hurt you. They want to help you.

☞ Pressuring you for sex and demanding sexual activities you feel uncomfortable doing are controlling behaviors—not acts of love.

☞ A history of family abuse conveys important information that is not to be ignored. Unless the person has worked through those past issues with counseling and/or treatment, the effects of abuse will continue to influence his or her behavior. Trying to be in a relationship with someone who has unresolved abuse issues is a huge undertaking and often ends badly, despite your best efforts.

A person may hold on to an abusive relationship because it seems better than being alone and left out of social activities with peers. An abuser adds to this sense of desperation by chipping away at the victim's self-esteem until the victim believes nobody else will ever love her or him. Abusers also confuse their victims by apologizing, declaring their love, and begging the other not to leave when they are in the "honeymoon" phase of the violence cycle described earlier. The honeymoon phase "hooks" the victim into believing the abuse will end without sacrificing the relationship. The pattern continues, however, until one or both partners seek help to break the cycle.

Get Help for Yourself

If you are in an abusive dating relationship, the following actions are recommended by the Family Violence Prevention Fund and author Barrie Levy, MSW.

- Take the emotional, physical, and/or sexual abuse seriously. Don't wait for it to progress.

- Stand up for yourself; set a boundary telling the abuser the violence must stop, particularly if the abuse is just beginning.

- Use caution. You risk more violence if you stand up for yourself without support from an adult or a friend. Before you speak up, be prepared to leave so as to escape the abuse. It is important to say what you feel and mean what you say. It is just as important to be safe when you say it.

- Tell your parents or a trusted adult. Let others help you.

- Say "No" clearly and repeatedly to sex if you do not want it. You always have the right to refuse and change your mind.

↝ Know the abuse is not your fault, nor is it deserved. Encourage the abuser to get help, remembering that you cannot make choices for anyone but yourself.

↝ Hurting yourself is not the answer. It is natural to feel down and angry when you are hurt, and you may think suicide is the only way out. It isn't. Use that anger instead to fuel the energy needed to take care of yourself. You do not have to stay in an abusive relationship no matter what the abuser tells you. Have faith that your life can get better.

↝ Don't be afraid to call the police or other authorities, or a domestic violence hotline.

↝ Take legal action when warranted.

↝ Find a counselor or support group.

↝ Do things for yourself that make you feel stronger and better able to cope with stress, like regular exercise, eating well, or taking self-defense classes.

↝ Avoid using alcohol and drugs. This temporary pain relief fogs your outlook when your thinking needs to be clear.

↝ Save money in an emergency fund and acquire or enhance job skills to reduce your financial dependence and increase your self-confidence.

Sometimes it takes outside intervention to motivate a teen to leave an addictive relationship.

Discovering Self Worth with Peer Support

"In those classes, I learned that I am worth something. I met and talked to other teens involved in violent dating relationships. It helped me so much to hear people my own age telling me that I didn't have to give up my body or my money to get some guy to love me. I learned that someone's going to love me just the way I am. I stopped seeing the guy, and I go to a counselor and attend a support group once a week.

"I am in tenth grade, living at home with my mom and stepdad. I don't want to date anybody right now. Sex comes with so much emotional baggage, and I was not ready for it. My goal is to become a lawyer or work for an insurance company.

"My advice to a teen in an abusive dating relationship is: Tell your family what is going on. They probably do not know. From there, get some type of counseling to help you get past that point where you think the abuse is something you deserve. I wore long sleeves and baggy clothes to hide the bruises and keep the abuse a big secret. Now I know I deserve better than that. Nobody deserves any kind of abuse."

Without the support of counseling, group therapy, and self-improvement efforts, you are likely to repeat abusive and codependent cycles in all your relationships. Leaving your abuser is a big step, but not the only one. Next, you learn to value yourself.

Stalking

Sometimes leaving an abusive situation and restoring your self-esteem is not enough to free yourself. Stalking is another form of abuse a person may resort to after a break-up. A stalker can be someone you know or a stranger. (Intimate-partner stalking accounts for 70 to 80 percent of all stalking cases.) In situations involving an intimate-partner stalker, know that if there has been violence in the relationship, the stalker is more likely to resort to violence again.

If someone is following and watching you and/or calling on the telephone repeatedly and hanging up without speaking, that is stalking. It is a crime—whether or not you know the person and whether or not you are threatened.

Experts believe the crime of stalking is under-reported. The legal definition of stalking varies from state to state, but the emphasis is on harassing behavior, following someone and/or issuing threats, and causing a person to fear for his or her safety.

Trusting your intuition is your first line of defense against a stalker. If you suspect that someone is following you, knows your schedule, and/or is sending anonymous notes or telephoning relentlessly, get more information about stalking and how to stay safe.

Experts say stalkers, like bullies, want a reaction from you. Your reactions make them feel as if they are engaged in some sort of relationship with you and that they are controlling you. Therefore, one way to discourage a stalker is to show no reaction to his or her presence or threats. While you show no reaction, however, do not deny the situation, hoping the stalker will just go away.

Instead of choosing a passive approach, take action. Tell your family, a friend, or trusted adult. Don't worry if they tell you it is just your imagination. Trust your gut. Contact a victim's assistance group. This may be a domestic violence prevention group or shelter, an abuse hotline, or crisis center. Such organizations' telephone numbers are typically listed in the emergency services or crisis hotlines section of your local telephone book. The professionals there will advise you regarding your next steps.

If the stalker is someone you know, end the relationship clearly. Say, "I'm sorry; I do not want to see you anymore." Do not say, "I have a boyfriend now," or, "I don't want a relationship right now." Give the stalker no hope of ever being friends with you, then say no more.

Avoid contact with the stalker. Take different routes to and from work and school. Carry a cell phone with you at all times. Ask for help from friends and family, and try not to show up anywhere alone. Get an answering machine and Caller ID to screen telephone calls. Rather than changing your phone number, ask your parents to order a second phone line and give that number only to those whom you trust. These are relatively low-cost safety precautions allowing you to keep in communication with the outside world via the second phone line. The stalker will reach only your answering machine on the line he knows to call. This helps relieve your stress while discouraging the stalker. Any messages left by the stalker help document the crime.

Keep your car locked. If someone follows you while driving, go directly to the police station, not to your home or the home of a friend. Document instances of stalking by logging the date, time, and places of incidents. Ask your employer and co-workers to help by changing shifts with you, screening calls for you at work and walking you to and from your car. Speak to a victim's assistance advocate, attorney, or police officer about the pros and cons of obtaining a restraining order and other legal actions.

Being stalked may feel as if you are held hostage in your own home. It can be frightening, depressing, and exhausting. These measures have helped end stalking in some cases. There is no way to be certain of a stalker's intentions, so it is vital to take any steps necessary to protect yourself.

Why Violence Happens

Varied and complex reasons are given for abusive behaviors between partners who started out loving each other. As mentioned in earlier chapters, children who grow up witnessing violence between their parents are deeply affected by those scenes and may believe it is normal, even expected, behavior. Other influences, such as movies, books, television, and newscasts that depict and glorify aggression, contribute to society's acceptance of power struggles between individuals.

A young man may feel peer and cultural influences to "be the boss" of his girlfriend rather than respecting her as his equal. Similar cultural trends may sway young girls to focus on pleasing their boyfriends and holding on to relationships no matter what.

Finding Balance

After summoning the courage to break up with your abuser and leave the relationship, you may feel empty inside, like a bottomless pit that cannot be filled. Getting over a broken heart is not easy, but the pain will pass. It takes time. You may feel sad and low on energy for a while. Your eating and sleeping habits may change, and you may think at times that you simply cannot go on without seeing or talking to your "ex" again.

A bad relationship can be treated like any other addiction. The temptation to see the person who is not good for you is similar to the desire to overeat, smoke, drink, abuse drugs, shop, steal, rage, or any other behavior you feel compelled to do even though you know it is self-destructive. Psychologists point out that each time you feel a temptation, and choose the right action instead of giving in, you increase your power over whatever is tempting you. If you are addicted to an abusive person, know that you can overpower your addiction. Then your choices are more likely to build, rather than tear down, your self-esteem.

Grief is natural after any loss, including the loss of a relationship—even an unhealthy one. You may go through stages of anger and disbelief or denial about the break-up, followed by a desire to bargain: "If only this or that had not happened, we would still be happy together."

It feels strange and scary to be suddenly alone after being consumed with the chaos and confusion of an abusive relationship. Talking about your feelings to your support group, friends, and counselor eases the pain. Professionals also can evaluate your need for further assistance, such as medication or different therapies, to cope successfully with the sadness and discomfort that often accompany going through any sort of transition.

Starting Over

Accepting the end of a relationship, though, means you get to start over. Keeping a journal of feelings, hopes, and dreams is both healing and inspiring. Later, when your energy returns, the ideas you have jotted down in your journal serve as a kind of treasure map for your new goals. Spending some time alone may be helpful at first, but don't become a hermit. When you are ready, reach out to others. Volunteer for a school or community project or get involved with others with whom you share common interests.

Spend time with friends who are supportive and help you feel good about yourself. Exercise every day—even a fifteen-minute walk can brighten your perspective and make you feel better. Take some extra time dressing and grooming yourself. Presenting your best appearance can lift your spirits. Keeping busy is an effective weapon in the battle against depression, fatigue, and obsessive thinking.

There is no timetable for mending a broken heart, but it does eventually heal. Working on yourself and developing (or rediscovering) your own interests will help you to feel more complete on your own, not as though a piece of you is missing unless you have your partner by your side. In reality, in healthy relationships there is no "better half," because both partners are already whole. You can lose that desperate need for another person to fill in the gaps inside you. Nurture your self-esteem, do the things that you enjoy, and begin the healthy habit of loving yourself.

When you are ready to toss your hat back into the dating arena, respect yourself and the progress you have made enough to consider only partners who demonstrate healthy behavior. Accept invitations from those who behave in a nonthreatening, supportive manner. Reject those who intimidate, boss, or criticize. Remember, harsh words often lead to hard punches.

"My boyfriend is older—twenty-two," says Deanna, a sixteen-year-old student at PACE Center for Girls, a private, nonprofit school for at-risk girls in Florida. *"At first, he just yelled at me, which I didn't like. But when he started hitting, it made me feel so low. I knew I deserved better. After he put me in the hospital, I promised myself I wasn't going to be with him, but I'm still scared I'm going to get hurt—like he'll come in through the window after me and get all up in my face again. He keeps telling me he loves me, but I know hitting somebody is no way to show love."*

The PACE (Practical, Academic, Cultural Education) Center for Girls, Inc., began in Jacksonville, Florida, in 1985 to respond to the needs of girls in the juvenile justice system. Based on its success, PACE has been replicated in communities throughout Florida and has received national recognition as a successful model.

Signs of a Healthy Relationship

Friends do not intimidate, criticize, or put down their friends in an effort to inflate their own position. They feel no need to do that because they are confident of their own self-worth. In fact, good friends and dating partners often brag about each other's achievements and talents. Anything can be complimented: an awesome solo performance at the school band concert, a funny story, homemade cookies shared at lunch, a precise pass thrown on the football field. It feels really good to be proud of each other and openly express that support instead of exchanging sarcastic put-downs.

Becoming a respectful listener is one of the most loving gifts you can bring to a friendship or dating relationship. Listening patiently without interrupting or judging may not always be easy, but it is always appreciated. Even when you do not agree, you can learn to listen and keep cool in the midst of heated discussions. This practice hones your communication skills and your ability to resolve potential conflicts before they escalate into full-blown arguments. You don't have to know the answer to the person's problem. Sometimes what a person needs most is simply to be heard. Some abusers say they sometimes strike when they feel frustrated with struggling to express something to another who seems unwilling to listen.

Building Communication Skills

When you need to be heard, keeping your voice low has the greatest impact, even when you feel strongly about making your point. Speaking with clarity may take some practice, especially if you developed the habit of being indirect and manipulative in the past. The conviction, not the volume, in your voice brings others' attention to what you are saying. On the other hand, others may want to "tune out" an offensive tone or a raised voice. They may want to ignore or distance themselves from dramatics like screaming, crying, pounding fists, and flinging objects. Think about the tantrum behavior observed in some two-year-olds, and ask yourself if that is how you wish to behave or see your partner behave.

Others respect your ability to be direct and honest without being cruel. These communication skills take time to build, but they will help you throughout your life in personal and professional associations. Using the "I" format helps you express what you feel without accusing the other person with "you" statements. "I was worried when you did not call," expresses your feeling. "You are unreliable and inconsiderate" sounds like an accusation. "I need help with this," is a message that differs vastly from "You expect me to do everything!"

When someone seems to be trying to provoke you with accusations, you can decide not to play that game. Responding with, "I'm sorry you feel that way," redirects the conversation and sometimes slows the current of anger that may be building. The statement is not an admission of guilt, nor does it express agreement. It simply says the other person has a right to his or her own feelings. Another comment that may temper an overreaction to some named fault, imagined or real, is "You may be right." This is also a successful defuser, a comment that deflates rather than inflames a tense situation. Again, it does not express agreement, only the possibility that the other person is right. It may calm down a person who is determined to convince you of something. To remove the fuse from a bomb keeps it from exploding. Defusing a verbal confrontation may keep the discussion from exploding into a big argument.

Accepting responsibility for yourself and letting others do the same brings honesty, trust, respect, and maturity to a healthy relationship. This means admitting when you are wrong, making amends, and working to stop repeating the offending action. Apologizing or promising to change, then continuing the behavior, is not acceptable. Words must be sincere and followed up with action.

It's okay to make mistakes. You don't have to try to be perfect for fear of repercussions or rejection by your friends or sweetheart. You can admit your doubts and fears. You don't have to try to be someone you are not.

Gestures, body language, and facial expressions need to be such that others feel safe and comfortable responding to you. The same is true both for your friends and intimate partners. If you feel intimidated by the way someone speaks to you, looks at you, or touches you, trust your intuitive senses and distance yourself.

If your partner needs to end the discussion and leave the room or the house, let him or her go. If you need to step outside or take a walk to cool off, go and do that. Even in the most harmonious relationships, people sometimes need a cooling-off period. It is healthy to recognize and act upon that need before words and actions are used in anger and later regretted.

Growing Without Growing Apart

Another sign of a healthy relationship is that it evolves into an encouraging partnership, allowing the growth and free expression of both partners. You need not fear changes because you trust each other, and you trust that you will be okay whether or not the relationship lasts. You don't need to trap or manipulate each other. You look forward to seeing each other and sharing your feelings about the events in your daily lives, without the need to check up on each other and worry about what your partner is up to when out of your sight. Letting the relationship take its natural course requires a delicate balance between loving yourself and loving your partner.

Cooperative Parenting

For teens who are parents, living together or apart, it is important to practice healthy parenting for the safety, security, and well-being of your child. Being courteous and cooperative can be difficult at times when the relationship is strained. But the payoff for parents who try to function as a team where the child is concerned is raising a happier, calmer, more confident child.

The distribution of parental responsibilities, including household and childcare tasks, should be fair to all concerned—divided as equally as possible. Family decisions need to be agreed upon together, not commanded by one person with no input from others in the family.

A child-support check every month is important, but it is not the only thing the child needs from either parent.

Healthy parents do not use their children to coerce or manipulate each other into any type of concession—sexual, financial, legal, or social. They strive to be respectful, nonviolent role models for their children, rather than exhibiting a "Do as I say and not as I do" attitude. By showing, not dictating, healthy behaviors, you give the child a great gift—the chance to break the cycle of abuse and create a brighter future for all.

Friend in Need

If you have a friend who is being victimized in a relationship, you can help her or him find the strength needed to break free. Counselors suggest the following actions.

- Ask questions about any bruises or other signs of abuse you notice. A person who is being hurt in a relationship may feel ashamed and/or to blame for the abuse. He or she may feel isolated with nobody to talk to, so don't wait for the victim to confide in you.

- Listen to your friend without judgment or strong reaction. A nonjudgmental attitude will keep the lines of communication open. Never gossip about the situation with other peers, although it may be appropriate to tell a trusted adult what is happening. Do not try to handle a dangerous situation by yourself; you do not have the skills a professional counselor offers. Understand that your friend may go back and forth trying to decide about leaving the relationship. Try to be patient with this process and continue honoring the strength and wisdom your friend shows in each choice.

↝ Help create a safety plan. Point out that your friend is not to blame for the abuse. Your reassurance can help balance the abuser's pattern of shaming and blaming the victim. Emphasize the need for staying safe. Help devise a safety plan of action that assesses the level of force the abuser uses, recognizes signs of an impending attack, and provides an escape route and safe shelter when it is necessary to leave. Together, make a list of local resources and emergency phone numbers.

↝ Encourage your friend to tell a parent or other trusted adult what is happening, and to find a counselor and/or group therapy. Talk to your friend's parents about the abuse. Don't assume they know about it. Sometimes, it is very difficult to discuss such things with your own parents but can be easier to talk to a friend's parents.

↝ Continue to support your friend and be there to listen after the break-up. It takes time to move on after being in a violent relationship. Knowing that someone else cares reinforces your friend's commitment at times when he or she feels weak and needy, wanting to return to the familiarity of the abusive relationship.

↝ If you become frightened or frustrated, get support. Educate yourself about dating violence. Don't neglect your own life to worry and obsess about your friend. You both need support during this fragile time.

Breaking the Cycle of Violence

The mission statement for Men Overcoming Violence (MOVE) includes this belief: "No one is born violent or abusive. We live in a society that teaches us that violence is often rewarded. Violence is a learned behavior that can be unlearned."

Recognizing the need to stop being abusive and to stop accepting abuse in your own relationships begins your life anew as a fully functioning person. Helping a friend come to the same awareness is another commendable achievement. From that point, opportunities abound if you wish to get involved with helping such organizations. In this way, the commitment to stop the violence widens the circle of healing even more, so that society and people all over the world benefit.

Organizations like The Empower Program, based in Washington DC, provide curriculum for schools such as "Owning Up" and "Stepping Up." In addition, Los Angeles-based LACAAW develops and distributes innovative school curricula worldwide through In Touch With Teens and Teen Abuse Prevention (TAPNet) programs. Each age-appropriate curriculum includes information, skits, ideas for artwork and murals promoting peaceful relationships, and a full spectrum of resources for teens in middle and high schools, as well as school guidance counselors, teachers, administrators, and parents.

There are many national, regional, and local resources that have been set up to provide help and hope for abused and abusive individuals. If you or someone you know has been abused, there is assistance and support for you. No longer ignoring or minimizing the effects of abusive relationships, men and women join in community spirit to correct the behaviors and heal the wounds. They respond to protect not only their sons and daughters, but all teens and families, because everyone's help is needed to build a safer world.

Glossary

adolescence   The period of development between childhood and adulthood.

alienate   To become unfriendly or indifferent; to estrange or dissociate from another.

berate   To scold harshly.

body language   Gestures and posture that reflect how one feels.

boundaries   Points at which values are to be respected and not violated.

codependency   A personality disorder, characterized by a loss of self, in which other people's needs are considered primary. The pattern can lead to anger, resentment, burnout, depression, addiction, and stress-related illness.

cognitive   Relating to processes for acquiring knowledge.

crisis   A situation of extreme change, which is typically dangerous.

date rape   Forced sex between two people who know each other.

detach   To separate oneself from another, physically and/or mentally.

domestic violence   Violence among family members or others who live together.

emotional abuse Shaming, criticizing, and other verbally abusive behaviors, including inattentiveness and neglect.

emotional blackmail Manipulation of a desired response from another by using emotional appeals and "guilt-tripping."

emotional support Listening to or encouraging someone regarding his or her feelings.

exploitation The act of using something or someone selfishly and unethically, usually for financial gain.

harassment Persistent annoyance that may become threatening and dangerous.

instincts Strong impulses, typically urging action, felt within you.

intimate partner Someone with whom you share sex and other intimacies.

intuition Understanding or insights that seem to emerge apart from rational thought.

isolation State of being apart from others, especially friends and family.

mirror work A technique used by mental health counselors to help clients build self-esteem and a positive self-image.

motivation Sense of eagerness and excitement about learning, trying, or performing a task.

peer group A group of friends or classmates of common age or interests.

peer pressure Motivation by the approval of others to do or act as they demand.

positive reinforcement Praise for action or achievement that is positive in any way.

psychotherapy Psychological counseling and treatment of mental, emotional, and nervous disorders.

self-esteem One's feelings of confidence or personal worth.

sexuality Sexual drives, or identity; interest in sex.

sexually transmitted disease (STD) Any disease transmitted from person to person through sexual contact.

Where to Go for Help

In the United States

Center for the Prevention of Sexual and Domestic Violence
2400 45th Street, #10
Seattle, WA 98103
(206) 634-1903
Web site: http://www.cpsdv.org
E-mail: cpsdv@cpsdv.org

The Empower Program
1312 8th Street NW
Washington, DC 20001
(202) 882-2800
Web site: http://www.empowered.org
E-mail: empower@empowered.org

Family Violence Prevention Fund (FVPF)
383 Rhode Island Street, Suite 304
San Francisco, CA 94103-5133
(415) 252-8900
Web site: http://www.fvpf.org
E-mail: fund@fvpf.org

National Coalition Against Domestic Violence
P.O. Box 18749
Denver, CO 80218
(303) 839-1852
Web site: http://www.ncadv.org

PACE Center for Girls of Hillsborough County
7402 56th Street North, Suite 306
Tampa, FL 33617
(813) 988-PACE

SafeNetwork
731 K Street, 3rd Floor
Sacramento, CA 95814
(916) 443-2017
Web site: http://www.safenetwork.net

In Canada

National Clearinghouse on Family Violence
Health Promotion and Programs Branch
Health Canada
Jeanne Mance Building
Address Locator 1907D1
Tunney's Pasture
Ottawa, ON K1A 1B4
(800) 267-1291
(613) 957-2938
Web site: http://www.hc-sc.gc.ca/hppb/familyviolence/
        bilingual.htm

Canadian Resource Center for Victims of Crime
141 Catherine Street, Suite 100
Ottawa, ON K2P 1C3
(613) 233-7614

Victims for Justice
P.O. Box 22023
3079 Forestglade Drive
Windsor, ON N8R 2H5
(519) 972-0836
Web site:
http://www.wincom.net/vfj/Workplaceharass&viol.htm

Hot Lines

Al-Anon/Alateen
(888) 4AL-ANON

Childhelp USA National Child Abuse Hotline
(800) 4-A-CHIILD

Children of the Night
(800) 551-1300

Kids Help (in Canada)
(800) 668-6868

National Abuse Hotline
(800) 799-SAFE

Rape, Abuse, Incest National Network (RAINN)
(800) 656-HOPE

Runaway Hotline
(800) 621-4000

Web Sites

Help4Teens
http://www.help4teens.com

Los Angeles Commission on Assaults Against Women
http://www.lacaaw.org

MOVE Program
http://www.menovercomingviolence.org

SafeNetwork
http://www.safenetwork.net/teens/safety.html

The Safe Horizon Website
http://www.safehorizon.org

For Further Reading

Adler, Patricia A., and Peter Adler. *Peer Power: Preadolescent Culture and Identity*. New Brunswick, NJ: Rutgers University Press, 1998.

Alateen Members and Sponsors, *Courage to Be Me: Living with Alcoholism*. Virginia Beach, Virginia: Al-Anon Family Group Headquarters, Inc., 1996.

Cook, Karin, *What Girls Learn: A Novel*. New York: Pantheon Books, 1997.

Covey, Sean. *The 7 Habits of Highly Effective Teens: The Ultimate Teenage Success Guide*. New York: Simon & Schuster, 1998.

Kindlon, Dan, Ph.D, Michael Thompson, Ph.D, and Teresa Barker. *Raising Cain: Protecting the Emotional Life of Boys*. New York: The Ballantine Publishing Company,1999.

Kreiner, Anna. *In Control: Learning to Say No to Sexual Pressure*. New York: The Rosen Publishing Group, 1997.

Levy, Barrie, MSW. *In Love & In Danger: A Teen's Guide to Breaking Free of Abusive Relationships*. Seattle, WA: Seal Press, 1993.

McGoldrick, Monica. *You Can Go Home Again: Reconnecting with Your Family*. New York: W. W. Norton & Company, Inc., 1995.

Scott, Sharon. *How to Say No and Keep Your Friends: Peer Pressure Reversal for Teens and Preteens*. Amherst, MA: Human Resource Development Press, 1997.

Index

About the Author

Carlene Cobb is a Florida-based freelance writer with a special interest in social and family issues and public health concerns.

616.85
Cob
1003000938618
18.96

Cobb, Carlene
Coping with an abusive
relationship

DATE		ISSUED TO

616.85   10030000938618
Cob

Cobb, Carlene
Coping with an abusive relationship